# FIFTY YEARS WITH SCOTTISH STEAM

Alan G. Dunbar is well known to observers of the
Scottish railway scene. For many years he has been
a contributor to various publications for railway
enthusiasts, where his writings have given pleasure
to many. He has also written a profile of the Caley
4-4-0s and is an authority on that line. His other
particular enthusiasm is the Great North of
Scotland Railway.

   This volume brings together some recollections of
almost fifty years of his now unique railway
associations. These recapture an era when
Glasgow was the greatest locomotive engineering
centre in Europe. Beginning with the North
British Railway, then with the Caley, his working
experiences were to continue through L.M.S.R.
and L.N.E.R. control until the twilight years of
steam in Britain. His researches since retirement
have thrown new light on the history of Scottish
locomotives as well as railway practice on Scottish
lines.

# *fifty years with* SCOTTISH STEAM

Alan G. Dunbar

*and*

I. A. Glen

BRADFORD BARTON

FRONTISPIECE

At Ardlui on the West Highland line K2 2–6–0 No. 61764 *Loch Arkaig* works an S.L.S. excursion in 1961; here it waits for a Class 5 with a Fort William – Glasgow (Queen Street) train to clear the section.

[C. H. Robin]

*ISBN 0 85153 427 9*
*copyright © Alan G. Dunbar*
*set and printed by CTP Ltd for Top Link Ltd*
*for the publishers*
D. BRADFORD BARTON LTD
*Trethellan House · Truro · England*

# CONTENTS

# PREFACE

This volume brings together some of my recollections of over fifty years' association with Scottish railways. At the outset I must mention the numerous railway enthusiasts who by conversation or by letter have given enrichment to my own knowledge. I have warm memories of so many of them.

Articles which first appeared in the Journal of the Stephenson Locomotive Society form the basis for some of the chapters. I am most grateful to the Council of the Society for the permission to enlarge them for re-publishing. Material has also come from my contributions to the Journal of the Great North of Scotland Railway Society. Ian Allan have given permission for portions of my story 'A Night to Remember', which was first published in 'Railway World', to appear here.

A. Ernest Glen, a fellow enthusiast of over sixty years' acquaintance, A. G. Ellis and G. H. Robin have generously given photographs from their collections to accompany my reminiscences. Other photographs have come from Derek Cross, Hamish Stevenson and the W. E. Boyd Collection.

Dr I. A. Glen has assumed the responsibility of editor for these reminiscences. She has taken the opportunity to compile this volume by collating material from my railway papers. I am most grateful for her assistance.

Finally for their patience over the years I must thank my wife, son, and daughter who tolerated strange hours of work, plus my immersion in an absorbing hobby – railway history.

It is my sincere wish that they, with you, will enjoy my railway recollections.

A. G. Dunbar

# CHAPTER I

## Here Comes the Trainie!

LET US GO back to the years of the Great North of Scotland Railway, and let the 'trainies' run again along memory's tracks. I was born at Bucksburn in the parish of Newmills, and so my first railway experiences were from that area. The Great North quickly became a boyhood enthusiasm; its activities were always entertaining, and most of its staff were characters. The Great North was one of those lines which came to enjoy much popularity, albeit after a rather hectic past.

When I was at the stage of being known as a wee loonie, I used to spend about three months of the year with my Grandma Dunbar at Bankhead, near Aberdeen, and the house was very close to the G.N.S. main line to Keith.

Around 1912, the centre of railway attention was the working of the Highland engines over the Great North to Aberdeen, counterbalanced by the G.N.S. reciprocal workings to Inverness. The Highland Railway was responsible for the 9.08 a.m. and the 1.05 p.m. from Inverness, and returned from Aberdeen with the 2.20 p.m. and the 6.45 p.m., while the Great North engines took out the 3.30 a.m. and the 8.05 a.m. from Aberdeen, returning with the 11.05 a.m. and 3.35 p.m. from Inverness. Latterly the rosters were altered and a G.N.S. locomotive was on the

9.45 a.m. from Aberdeen instead of the old 8.05 a.m. train. On these runs it was usual to see the Highland's 'Small Bens' venturing into Great North territory. I remember that *Ben Hope, Ben Alisky, Ben Dearg, Ben Alder* and *Ben MacDhui* were frequent visitors to the Granite City in those years. When the through runnings began 'the hale place was telt aboot it for weeks afore'. One of the Inverness men was well known – 'the "Duke" he wis kent as – and he ran the first Hielan' engine doon tae Aberdeen, fan the trains sterted tae go doon wi' ae ingine a the wey. Tam Gordon wis a gey fine chiel an' fowk said he wis a gran' driver. The first day they gaed doon we wis a oot tae see hom gaun by, and Tam wis blawin' the whustle an' wavin's bonnet at a' the fowk. *Ben Alisky* wis the ingine he hid that day – and fan he cam up at nicht we wis oot again tae see him.'

A small notebook in my schoolboy hand dates back to 1914 or so, and it became a pleasurable chore to note the engine numbers and what is now of greater interest, the trains which the engines were hauling. One curious entry refers to *luggage* trains: this term was commonly used in Buchan for all goods trains. An old Cullen lady I met referred to things happening before or after the 'dinner-time luggage', that is the goods from Elgin which came in about lunch time. One day I noted No. 4, a 'Big Kitson' 4–4–0 of 1888 hauling cattle wagons – the vans being filled with 'bulls' – do not ask how I reached that conclusion. Then three luggage trains came along hauled by Nos. 82 of Class S, 99 and 109 of Class T, all 4–4–0s of the 1890's. On the up line, there were several passenger trains, Nos. 114 of Class V, 111 of Class T and 75 of Class Q; with the exception of No. 75 which had been built by Stephenson, all had come from Neilson. Meanwhile Nos. 9 of Class O, 34 of Class V, and 94 of Class T were working goods trains on the up line; (No. 9 came from Kitson, No. 34 was constructed at Inverurie and No. 94 was a Neilson engine). Such observations served to emphasise the versatility and variety of the Great North's little 4–4–0s.

For the young train spotter there was another advantage in living so close to the main line to Keith. This was the fact that periodically all the G.N.S. locomotives paid a visit to Inverurie works for a routine examination. This was an affair lasting a day or so; hence the engine concerned came to Kittybrewster shed (or 'Kitty' as we called it) one evening, ran up light to Inverurie the following morning and then came down again at night. If all was well it then went home. Thus it was possible if one waited long enough to see all the Company's engines, but No. 1 was elusive until 1918! This locomotive was one of the Class C 4–4–0s which came from Neilson in 1875. Around the close of the first War, No. 1 arrived to work the old Meldrum branch, and as she ambled twice weekly into Aberdeen, she became quite familiar to me.

Our lineside nights were little disturbed by the passage of trains, for there was remarkably little night time activity on the Great North. I mean by that, trains running between 11 p.m. and 5 a.m. Apart from shunting at Kittybrewster, Keith or Waterloo in Aberdeen, there were only six regular trains between those hours on the whole system: these were

11.30 p.m.: Kittybrewster to Keith: goods
12.20 a.m.: Kittybrewster to Elgin: goods
3.30 a.m.: Aberdeen to Keith: passenger
4.35 a.m.: Aberdeen to Keith: goods
12.30 a.m.: Keith to Aberdeen: goods
4.45 a.m.: Aberdeen to Fraserburgh: goods

After the outbreak of the First War, however, this peaceful situation was shattered and many and various were the trains run at night in connection with naval establishments in the North. It was pitiful to watch the elderly G.N.S. 4–4–0s struggle along with a 'Jellicoe' coal train of forty wagons in filthy weather – but like the Buchan chiels, they were dour craturs and they eventually got there! It was amazing how these small locomotives managed to perform such tasks.

About 1915, the jottings become more explicit. No. 75 of Class Q of 1890 was on the 9.45 a.m. from Elgin to Aberdeen for a week, while the 6.45 p.m. express from Aberdeen to Elgin was run by No. 77 which had worked up on the 2.20 p.m. with its driver the 'weel kent' Alexander Davidson of Elgin. He was better known as 'The Masher', on account of his immaculate appearance. His locomotive for many years was No. 77, one of the Class Q engines of 1890 which had 6 ft. 6 in. coupled wheels and were known as the 'fleers'. Alec certainly saw to it that his engine was kept spotlessly clean.

Then there were the 'Subbies'. 'Subby' was the local term for 'sub-urban'. In 1887, when the Subbies were first run, much to the delight of the Aberdonians, they were called the 'Jubilee trainies'. They were put on for a month or so, but they became something of an institution and ran without a break until withdrawn by the L.N.E.R. in 1937. They served the needs of textile and papermill workers, of the quarrymen going to and from work, as well as the regular city commuters, schol-ars, students and shoppers going up to town. At holidays and on Satur-days, the Subbies took the townfolk out to the countryside for picnics and walks around Culter or other attractive rural areas near the city.

At first, the engines on the Subbies were little Kitson 0–6–0 tanks, some of which dated from 1884, but in 1893 bigger Neilson engines of the 0–4–4T type came along. I recall Nos. 85, 87, 90 and 92 of this Class

R with their extraordinary beat, which is hard to put into words, but resembled a shortened 'four in a bar'. It was recognisable a long way off, and once heard could never be mistaken for any other kind of locomotive. The drivers on the Subbies would open the regulator, and after about three or four canny revolutions of the wheels, the reversing lever was put into the cut-off position, and off the engine galloped – yes, galloped, as it perfectly describes their mode of running.

Then came the time when I could go out on Saturday nights – cherchez la femme – if you like. Today we would be known as 'teenagers' but then we were just 'loons' and 'quines'.

We used to travel into Aberdeen with the 6.1 p.m. from Bankhead arriving at 6.18 p.m., and we were very well behaved since many adults travelled into town with this train but the return journey was the one to which we looked forward. The last train which was about 10.40 p.m. was the one for the fun, and I can remember the porters at the Joint saying as we entered – "Mind noo lads – nae lichts pitten oot". This referred to the old-style oil lamps which could be knocked out by jumping up and giving them a sharp bump. In mixed company this was of course always done – *after* Schoolhill was passed – as there was a very officious inspector there who always turned up on Saturdays to stop "this roch wye o' gyaun on". Poor chiel – the train was hardly into the tunnel when the lamps went out and the ensuing uproar could have been heard far enough – at times the cushions were even thrown out of the windows by the bolder fellows.

At Woodside there was an adenoidal porter who, when shouting that station's name made it sound like nothing on earth – the nearest we get was "quinine" and if he was on duty on the Saturday night the whole train would yell "quinine" as it moved off. Naturally we didn't exactly like to do it when he could get hold of one or two of us, repaying our cheek with a hearty smack. All this hilarity cost only 6½d return – and when we were flush we splashed out on a first for 4d more. The Third Class return fare was the same as the First Class single fare.

When waiting to go into town in the morning, just before the 8.20 a.m. from Bankhead was due, there would be a shriek of a whistle as a locomotive came past the 'Auld School' at Stoneywood and round the curve would come the 6.20 a.m. from Keith going all out for Kittybrewster. A favourite Keith engine on this train about 1916 was No. 74, a Class O 4-4-0, and other times No. 81, a Class S with its jaunty 'bunnet' on the dome.

At this time all Great North engines were painted a light green, rather similar to the original L.N.E.R. green. This was lined out in black with white borders. The footplate margins were a dark purple brown with a white line along the edge itself. The axle boxes were given vermilion lines, while the letters G.N.S.R. were in gilt with red reveals. The coaching stock were turned out in brown and cream – the effect of the locomotive and carriage liveries being most harmonious. (After 1916 the engine livery was black with red lining).

During my annual holiday in 1923 I attempted to cover the whole of the Great North of Scotland Railway in less than a week. In fact the outings had to be completed in five days as on the Saturday I had to attend the wedding of a cousin of mine and of course in spite of my railway interests the family insisted that attendance was compulsory.

Although by September 1923 the G.N.S.R. was nominally part of the L.N.E.R. to all intents and purposes it was still the old company, and in spite of instructions from London or Doncaster it remained 'Great North' for many a year to come. Such documents as came from these L.N.E.R. outposts in the south had little effect, if any, in G.N.S. territory. Staff kept to their usual paths, and officialdom just had to acquiesce.

To travel over the Great North in such a short time as five days called for a lengthy examination of the timetable, and when this had been completed I found to my dismay that the service was rather poor as far as the railway enthusiasts were concerned. The exercise was going to take some ingenuity and patience. This first day was the biggest bite of the cherry, as will be seen. An early start was unavoidable – a 4.35 a.m. departure from Aberdeen – without any breakfast, but at least I was staying in the town! With the G.N.S.R. locomotive No. 48 *Andrew Bain* in the van, the train set off for Keith. This engine was one of the Class F types, built by the North British Locomotive Company in 1920, and it survived L.N.E.R. and B.R. takeovers until 1955. First light was breaking as we came up the valley of the Don making for Huntly, and Cairnie Junction. An hour or so was spent at Keith, the crisp September air soon made me hurry for some breakfast before catching the train for Elgin via Rothes. This time the engine was No. 23 of the T class, another of the Great North's ubiquitous 4–4–0s constructed by Neilson & Company in 1896. It continued to run until 1950.

There are some sharp inclines about Rothes but we came into Elgin at 8.30 a.m. There was time to explore the station and yard before catching the local to Lossiemouth for an eleven minute run! This was in fact the first line to open in the area – the Morayshire Railway of 1851. Then back to Elgin I came, to travel along the coast through the now vanished stations of Calcots, Urquhart, Garmouth, Fochabers, Fort Gordon, Buckpool, Buckie, Portessie, Findochty, Portknockie, Cullen, Tochieneal and Portsoy to Tillynaught Junction. In those years most of these places were fishing harbours, and volumes of perishable traffic came the way of the Great North at its stations on that route. The engine on the train that day was No. 52 *Glen Grant,* which was another member of the Class F of 1920. I well recall the breathtaking entry into Cullen with its curving viaduct above the bay and its high embankments – one of the few noteworthy civil engineering features on its system.

At Tillynought I took the train up the branch line to Banff. On that route there were once two drivers and two firemen. There was also a cleaner at Banff who was on perpetual night shift (What would the Unions say to that?) – his tasks being to keep the fire on as well as to clean the engine. Class 43 or K locomotives were on that line; they had a lot of brass work which was kept so well polished that it shone. They were like a Victorian granny with her best bonnet on, full of stately charm, but lacking in muscle power! The trains had four wheel coaches; a journey on them felt as though they had square wheels, or else ran over the ballast!

Then I returned to Tillynaught for a respite and a bite of lunch. Few Great North stations had refreshment rooms but there was always a local bakery where one could find a fresh roll. In the early afternoon, I set off again for Keith, and from there worked back to Inverurie where, around teatime, I broke my journey in order to sample the branch line via Lethanty to Old Meldrum. This was the route frequented in days past by an ancient locomotive which was known to the travelling public as 'Meldrum Meg'. Aberdeen was reached in time for supper, and I had already covered about a quarter of the Great North's tracks.

The day after, the programme was easier, encompassing the line to Ballater, and the branches in the Peterhead area. The 'right away' came at 8.05 a.m. when I caught the train for Ballater. Again the weather was typically 'Indian Summer' and the country was at its best with the heather in flower on the Moor of Dinnet and with the sparkling river glimpsed between the bushes and dark green pine trees at Banchory. What an attractive and majestic route that line was! Its closure was a missed opportunity both for tourism and for railway preservationists.

All too soon I was back in the Silver City, and at lunchtime an hour had to be put in before the train left for Peterhead. On this sortie we sauntered through the bare Buchan countryside which was then golden with harvest fields to Ellon and Maud Junction. After about three hours, for we stopped at every station on the way, we at last came down the coast to Peterhead with its bustling fishing harbour full of steam drifters. Time had to be tolerated before there was a train back to Ellon. There I had to spend a further hour before I journeyed via

Cruden Bay to Boddam. At that time Cruden Bay was advertised as the Great North's seaside resort, with its golf course, beaches, and tramcars to convey guests from the station to the railway's imposing Victorian hotel. But Cruden Bay never achieved the popularity of the Caley's Gleneagles or the Sou' West's Turnberry. We jogged along the coast past the Bullers o' Buchan, remarkable rocky stacks, which gave their name to a small station, and so to Boddam. The veteran 4-4-0 No. 58 was in front. This class M from Neilsons had joined the Great North as far back as 1875, and served the railway for over half a century. Two hours had to be whiled away at Boddam, but as the weather was glorious it was no hardship. In the early evening the return from Boddam began, and Aberdeen was reached shortly after 9 p.m.

On the Wednesday a start was made from Aberdeen just before 7 a.m., and the Alford branch together with the line to Macduff were the chosen routes. I retraced my opening excursion up the valley of the Don as far as Kintore, to board the 'trainie' for Alford there. It was hauled by No. 40, another vintage locomotive of 1878, which was sporting a rather rustic looking tender cab. She took 40 minutes for the journey calling at Kenmay, Monymusk, Tillyfourie and Whitehouse en route.

On the way to Alford we were passed by the 9.55 a.m. from Boddam, which after many adventures and delays used to arrive at Kitty about 2.30 p.m. This train had the same engine for years, old No. 5 which was one of the Class N of 1887; it had the doubtful honour of being one of the two locomotives to be built at Kittybrewster. All the parts were bought in from a variety of locomotive builders, and No. 5 together with No. 6 is reputed to have been put together in the yard outside! Needless to say, this attempt to construct locomotives at Kitty was never repeated. Before the First World War the Boddam goods shunted at every station, and patiently waited while a farmer would load or unload a horse or a reaping machine. Meantime all the gossip of the countryside was exchanged with the train crew, as this was prior to the eight hour day, when the enginemen never seemed in a hurry to get home.

Once again the weather was at its fairest and I had ample opportunity of savouring Donside with its productive farmlands and woodlands which gave so much traffic to the Great North.

Having returned to Kintore, there was now an hour or so in which to relax before the train for Macduff appeared. With a wave of the green flag, and a shrill blast on the whistle, off we went passing Inverurie works on the way, and branching northwards at Inveramsay to follow part of the Ythan Valley, and then the Deveron to Macduff. The journey took about two hours, but the visit to Macduff was very brief – just five minutes – scarcely time to look across to neighbouring Banff where I had been on the Monday. I had to eat a 'piece' on the train that day. By mid-afternoon, I was in Aberdeen once more. This was much too early for a young enthusiast to call it a day, so the evening was spent in taking trips on the subbies from Aberdeen to Culter and back, to sample everything the Great North had to offer.

When Thursday came along, a major excursion was in view – a trip to Boat of Garten which lay in the most westerly corner of the Great North's system. An outing to the Boat or to any of the stations en route was a favourite one with Aberdonians in pre First War years. It was run twice weekly. Dufftown was a particularly popular stopping-off point.

So after an early breakfast on the Thursday I was on board the train at Aberdeen at 7.45 a.m. Thence we wound our way to Huntly and Keith, then along the valley of the Fiddich to Dufftown and Craigellachie Junction. Although trains of excursionists frequented the route, particularly in summer, the principal traffic served the distilleries – every siding was replete with wagons bringing in barley, coals and timber, and taking away casks of malt whisky. The air was redolent with the aroma of peat, of malt and of distillery wastes. It is bonnie country from Craigellachie up to Grantown. The country folk were bringing the harvest home with horse-drawn reapers in the fields. After Nethybridge the track ran parallel with the Highland's line (from Forres over Dava Moor) for three miles into Boat of Garten. And many were the races between Highland and Great North trains that took place over these rails, although there was no racing the day I ventured to Boat of Garten. Shortly before lunch the 'Boat' came into view. The station was a Highland one, the signals commanding the Great North were Highland, and the latter had to be content with its own shed and turntable at a discreet distance from the station proper.

After about two hours in Boat of Garten the return was made, and by 5.15 I was in Aberdeen after the lengthiest journey over its home terrain which the Great North had to offer – over 130 miles for 2s 6d return!

On the final day, I had to retrace my steps as far as Maud Junction in order to visit Fraserburgh (or 'the Broch' as it was known in the North East) to tour the St. Combs branch. I joined the train in Aberdeen at the civilised hour of 8.30 a.m., and just after ten was in Fraserburg itself. The St. Combs engines had cow-catchers as the line was unfenced, but their pace was so leisurely that it was suggested they should also have such devices at the rear! There was only one station on this branch, Cairnbulg, and after a half hour pause at St. Combs, the return journey began. There was ample time in Fraserburg to go to the harbour, explore the sidings and find some lunch, and by 3 p.m. I was back in the Granite City again.

The cost of the exercise was minimal. As a railwayman with the Caley, I enjoyed concessionary fares; when I set foot in Great North territory, a call to a friend at Kittybrewster ensured that the concession would also apply there and hence my outings were done at *half* the single fare. The entire programme probably cost less than three pounds.

Although there were a few early starts, most of the outings finished early in the day: the reason was that many of the branches had no evening return service to Aberdeen, the locomotives on several of the routes such as the Alford or Old Meldrum routes being 'stabled' overnight at these stations.

I remember the extraordinary variety of architecture in the stations, in such details as the wooden valances on the roofs – all the result of the whims of local contractors. A lasting regret is that lack of finance forbade my having a camera – hence a notebook and pencil had to suffice.

# CHAPTER TWO

## A 'Prentice Hand

I SUPPOSE LIKE MOST small boys in the old age of steam, I wanted to be an engine driver, an ambition which many youngsters shared in those far-off days. Now it is all so different – engine driving is just a routine mechanical job, and small boys want to become astronauts or pop singers instead. But back in 1914 how many realised their youthful ambition to join the railways? I was fortunate to realise mine and to spend my years working among steam engines. I never once regretted it. Hard, dirty, heavy, even cruel work it was at times, but the fascination of the steam locomotive at its zenith made up for it all.

In mid 1916, at 14 years of age, I began work with the North British Railway at Cowlairs in what was called the 'General Stores' Department. 'General' was an admirable description for it, and you might even have found the proverbial needle or an anchor among the wealth of materials of all kinds which lay on its shelves. After all, the North British ran a fleet of steamers, and nautical gear was also in evidence. My work was simple – as the last one in, I was a roving all-purpose helper at the beck and call of everyone from the stores superintendent J. J. Smith down to the lad who was my immediate superior.

The Chief Clerk was a Calvinistic Scot named Storey. When girl mployees were introduced to his office, he considered it to be the most etrograde step to take place in Scotland since the Union of the Crowns! We also had one of Springburn's remarkable characters in the North British stores – Andrew Dougal, or 'Sir Andrew' as he was known. His work consisted principally of rope splicing of both hemp and wire, and he was an acknowledged expert at this. Everyone said Andra was daft, or at least not quite all there, but it was always open to doubt just how far off the beam he really was.

The real bosses in the stores, however, were the two brothers Bell who took charge of the stores train. This was an institution that journeyed all over the N.B. system each month, calling at every station and yard, leaving the stores required, and picking up all returned, surplus or waste materials. It consisted of three vans of the passenger brake type, plus several open and closed wagons all 'piped' for braking; this curious assemblage carried a staff of five, if I remember correctly. The drivers of the Stores Special were always Eastfield men, and there was a regular guard on it as well.

After a short period in the actual store I joined John Jarvie, who was the analytical chemist in the N.B. laboratory. My job was to wash the lab equipment, and to make myself useful. Mr Jarvie was a 'perjink' body – in other words he was rather fastidious and straight-laced. He wore an old fashioned gladstone wing collar, a sober dark grey suit, and lived in Bishopbriggs, which was a fancy place in which to reside in those days. It was far from tenements or pubs, and could fairly be described as a country retreat. It was particularly popular with Glaswegians who had made good.

My work was only interesting because I was sent on various trips in connection with it. Not exactly thrilling, but at least I got out and about on the North British lines. There were jaunts to water columns to fill up big Winchester bottles with samples of water for analysis; to engine sheds to collect coal, oil or other materials; and to the works for samples of paint, varnish, or red lead. These tasks occupied my days, and gave me a first-rate opportunity of going round the whole system.

Mr. Jarvie was also responsible for the wagon grease-making plant that was housed in the stores department at Cowlairs. The grease was a compound of yellow soap, stearine, and what were termed fatty acids. The yellow soap had been introduced many years earlier to add a touch of caustic soda to the mixture – ostensibly to prevent the Poles and Lithuanians in Lanarkshire from taking the grease out of the wagons at the pitheads and goods yards, in order to use it as cooking fat. This story may be open to question, but there was a lot of prejudice against these unfortunate refugees from Eastern Europe who made their way to

Central Scotland and found work in the coal mines and steel works of Lanarkshire.

Some pressure was put on me to go to the Technical College and take a course in chemistry, but I hedged about this for so long, that eventually Mr. Jarvie told me that if I did not accept I would have to go back to the stores again! But, that same day I was sent over to St Rollox works with some samples of steel to have them examined on the Caledonian Railway's testing equipment. Being utterly fed up with the prospect of being a reluctant analytical chemist I sought out the Works Manager. I walked into Mr. Irvine Kempt's office as bold as brass, and asked for a job in the erecting shop. Due to the First War exigencies, apprentices were commencing at 15 years of age instead of the more usual 16 years. Mr. Kempt looked at me in amazement, but he was kind enough to ask me about my reasons for wanting to enter a locomotive erecting shop. The upshot of this impromptu interview was that he told me to go back to Cowlairs, and that he would let my superior know – which he did, three weeks later. Thus I came to shake the dust of Cowlairs off my feet. From now on I was going to be a Caley man; and the first step towards the realisation of a boyhood ambition had been taken.

Up in Springburn, St. Rollox was always known as 'The Caley' and it still is that to many. It employed about 3500 people. To me it was a completely new world. As I lived in Maryhill, I caught the 5.10 a.m. tramcar – a white car – round Bilsland Drive, which in those days had very little housing except for a cluster at Possilpark near the old Saracen Foundry. Work commenced at 6 a.m. and it was a long day as I arrived home well after 6.30 in the evening. It was a rude awakening after the shelter of school days, and the gentility of my previous employment!

When one entered the St. Rollox works gate, there were large boards with hooks on which checks hung; you picked up your check and took it to the department where one was working. There you dropped the check into a slotted box in the charge of the watchman for the erecting shop – in my day a veteran with a beard called 'Auld Barney', who looked like Methuselah. At six sharp when the horn blew, Barney shut the 6 a.m. slot, and opened the 6.15 a.m. one. You were then liable to be 'quartered', and at 6.15 the slot for 6.30 was opened and you were 'half houred'. At 9.45 a.m. or 2 p.m. after the lunch break, you had to be on time, or you were out. Of course in the morning there was an institution known as "Hae'in a mornin'", which meant that the individual concerned had a lie-in and came out as fresh as paint at 9.45 a.m. The squads in the erecting shop, especially in the tender lye, had arrangements for perhaps two of their number at a time to have a job inside the tank, and a lump of red hot iron would be brought from the

[ 18 ]

forge as a 'heater' and placed therein to take off the chill if the day was cold. This made the tank or boiler shell quite comfortable for a snooze until 8.30 a.m.

My check number when I began was 124, and this had some prestige, for the men associated the numbers with Caley 'ingines', as they called them. Of course, No. 124 had been *Eglinton,* a celebrated 4-4-0 of 1886, and a named locomotive carried much more honour than one without. Considerable resentment was felt that 903, which was the number of the prestigious *Cardean,* was the check allotted to a chap who was a sweeper in the brass shop! That the famous engine was thus dishonoured was a source of humiliation to many.

My first morning in the works was a depressing experience – the rows of gaunt, silent and stripped engines, the gas light, and the clutter of wheels, tanks, domes and other bits and pieces. The strangeness of it all made a lasting impression on me. Apprentices usually started in the fitting or turning shop but I went straight away to the erecting shop, and found myself in the stores again. This was done to familiarise the boys with the stocks of materials (bolts, studs etc) and tools which were kept there. There was always a cheery fire in a huge stove, and some privacy and peace from the hubbub and clangour outside. After George Kelly, the storeman who was in charge, had given me a mug of real erecting shop tea – black, sweet and horribly smoked but mighty good on a cold morning, I began to feel more at home.

The work at the stores was simple – men and boys came up to the store window for material with a 'line', and having supplied them with what was wanted, the line was duly marked with the number of the 'doocot' or section from which the item had been removed. The line was then sent over to Johnnie Grey, the stores clerk, so that he could check his stock cards. George Kelly sat on a high stool and kept an eye on us – when someone came for, say, studs 3 inches by ¾ inch, he would sing out "Row twa, – aboot sax alang, fower up frae the flair". Naturally I thought this was wonderful until after about six weeks in the store I found I could do it myself!

Around the store stove the erecting shop charge hands foregathered, and talked – their discussions ranging over the war, politics, the inevitable "fitba" and horseracing. Then there was the usual gossip about engines or the Company.

A frequent visitor to the store was Charlie McGill. He had been a cleaner in a shed, but had lost an arm, and came to the Erecting Shop as a Messenger. His specialities were stories of pub brawls, and there were highly entertaining, at least to my young ears.

After the initial ten or twelve weeks in the store an apprentice with the Caley went into the tender lye, and usually stayed there six to seven months. Here one was left to pick up the skill of using tools – the hammer, chisel and file – and many were the sore knuckles I had before the knack was acquired. It was tough work for a youngster attempting to dress down a tender frame with a hammer and chisel, and the racket was deafening. In addition, every 'green hand' was sent for 'a long stand' or some similar 'gowk's errand', but once this was over, and a good laugh had at the lad's expense, he was accepted as one of the shop. My experience of this leg-pulling was to swallow a tale that one of the fitters wanted large potatoes – and I actually brought three from home only to have them thrown at me. But if you failed to take all this teasing in good part you were ribbed all the more.

Working on the tenders was rather monotonous. After all there was little to choose between one and the other, and again I was glad that after only five months I was shifted from the tender lye to Pit 18, then under Harry Rennie. Pit 18 had something of an aura for it dealt with the 'big' engines. When I went to it in 1918 the three engines at the pit were No. 903 *Cardean*. No. 943 and No. 184.

In 1906 *Cardean* had been constructed at St. Rollox, being one of six similar 4-6-0s which became known as the 903 class. Every schoolboy had heard of *Cardean* in these days – even if they knew none other. No. 943 was one of the Highland River class acquired by the Caley in 1915, which had been constructed by R. W. Hawthorn Leslie & Co. Ltd. of Newcastle-upon-Tyne. These had the express passenger livery, and No. 943 was a Perth engine. On the other hand No. 184 had been St. Rollox built and belonged to the 179 class of 4-6-0 engines of 1914. This engine was also based at Perth in those years. The 179 class was a just superheated version of the 908 class, but had side window cabs. Their driving wheels were only 5 ft. 9 ins. and there were officially designated goods locomotives, although they were also on passenger workings in their early days.

Harry Rennie was a wee fellow, but he had graduated to being a charge hand from years of work on the new engines, and this carried a certain cachet among the shop hands. Harry had been at the building of many famous Caledonian locomotive classes – notably the 139's – and he had an excellent method of giving his apprentices a thorough training. Instead of allowing them to become general knock-abouts for any of the six journeymen in his squad, the lad was assigned to work for a period with each in turn, and thus, since the men all tackled different jobs, they gained wide experience, hence Harry's system was very much to the youngster's advantage.

I was sent first to help old Pete Andrews, who saw to the fitting of boiler mountings and all work of this nature, due to his age and a slight infirmity. One of my first jobs was to sit astride the boiler of the Caledonian giant *Cardean*, watching old Pete attending to the routine maintenance of the safety valves. Then I moved on to other tasks, such as the fitting of axle boxes or pistons with the younger men.

The Erecting Shop consisted of three long bays, numbered 1, 2 and 3. As you entered No. 1 from the main passageway you saw three roads for locomotives before you. Those at the sides were over pits, while the centre one was floored and was usually piled up with axle boxes and other locomotive gadgetry.

The pits themselves were split up to hold three engines each, and each pit section was under a chargehand. The number of men at each pit varied according to the type of locomotive being repaired and there was always some distinction in working on 'new' or 'big' engines. Greater prestige for instance was attached to pits 17 and 18, where the Caledonian 4-6-0s were serviced, than say to pit 3 where Dunky Turner repaired nothing but 'pugs' – 0-4-0 saddle tanks being his speciality. Each bay had two overhead cranes, in charge of two cranemen and two slingers, who were among the busiest individuals in the whole shop.

At the time of the First War, the Chief Foreman at St. Rollox was Mr. Williamson, who had come from Inverurie, and was reputed to have married a daughter of William Pickersgill, the Caley's Locomotive Superintendent. He eventually left to go to Armstrong Whitworth. In charge of No. 1 shop was Alex Hallam, Jock Brough was in No. 2, and John Jamieson in No. 3. The foremen all wore the regulation bowler hat, which was de rigeur in those days – soft hats or, even worse, bare heads were unthinkable. Old John Harrower, who was the 'outside' Works Manager, had a half pot hat – a reminder of the old times when a railway official was considered a real personage. Jock Brough had moved up from the new engine building pits, and was followed as new engine builder by Willie Grant, an Elgin 'loon' who built the 956 class, Scotland's first major three cylinder locomotives.

All the pits in the Erecting Shop specialised in particular engines. Thus at pit No. 7 one found Alex Clements busily working on Dunalastair IIs and IIIs – nothing else. At pit 9, there was Will Sorbie whose sole employment was the maintenance of Dunalastair IVs of the saturated variety. The pride of the shop was to work at pits 2 and 11 with Will Grant and Willie Graham who built the new engines. Over in No. 3 shop, there were six tender lyes, where Jimmy Smith constructed the new tenders, and Bob Lewis repaired the bogie types.

One thing that struck anyone coming into the works was the vast number of third and fourth generation railway personnel who were in

St. Rollox. Some of their great grandfathers had started with the Garkirk & Glasgow, or the Glasgow, Paisley & Greenock Railways. Orfamily called Frew, whose forbears had been on the former line, haentered into the fourth generation to be employed by the Caley. It w:similar with many others – men could trace their railway ancestry bacto such companies as the Aberdeen Railway, the Scottish North Easern, or the Scottish Central. Charlie Herd, the chargehand at Pit 2who came from Perth, had stemmed from a great-grandfather who habeen a driver on the Dundee & Newtyle. John Ramage at Pit 27 was aelderly chap, whose brother James looked after the cylinder shop. Thewere proud of their grandfather, who had come from the Grand Junetion Railway to Greenock to work with Robert Sinclair, the Caleyfirst locomotive chief. Of course, this also applied to some extent to thother locomotive works in Springburn. When I travelled up in thmorning several of the men who worked in Atlas and Hydepark weron the tramcar; the man in charge of the cylinder fitting shop at Hydpark told me his great-grandfather had been with the firm when it w:first based in Finnieston near the River Clyde. Another group could laclaim to having fathers as drivers with the Caley. All of these men hastarted in the local shed, and came up to the works for the final year ctheir apprenticeship. Very often they remained at St. Rollox – the regular hours, particularly after the eight-hour day was introduced, were aattraction compared to the irregular shifts at a shed.

An example was Bill Crooks at Pit 24; he was the son of the celebrated Carlisle driver, Archie Crooks of 'Race to the North' fameAbout 1920, Bill went to take command of the new steaming shedbuilt just outside the erecting shop.

John Jackson at Pit 17 was an odd chap who seldom spoke and yehad the greatest experience of any chargehand – after serving hiapprenticeship with the Caley he had gone to work in HydeparkCrewe, Doncaster, Darlington, Swindon, and Cowlairs, before returning to the Caley. This was called 'gettin' eggsperience', and more othis anon.

All these longstanding relationships gave the whole works the air offamily and it was usually taken for granted that son would follow fathein the Company, although not always in the same job.

Many of the men were characters – one of the best known at StRollox was Davy Woods, the 'gaffer' for the general labourers. If therwas a more harassed individual in Springburn, no-one ever met himDavy had the whole burden of the works on his shoulders, and whesomeone would go to him to order a set of wheels or other requirements to be brought in from the yard, Davy would 'proper book it'

he booking consisted of scribbling something that was indecipherable
a worn notebook and yet the stuff was always delivered. One of
avy's men was in the Erecting Shop – Jock Sproul was his name – and
is job was to scrape down much of the engines' dirt; he had a special
uit made of canvas that he wore that was said to have all the filth on it
om Dugald Drummonds's time. This outfit was never cleaned, and in
ct the older hands in the shop averred that the suit had given out years
efore, and only the dirt remained!

A very prevalent habit among many of the men was one that is never
en today – chewing tobacco. Small wonder that the tramcars carried
e notice 'no spitting'. John Ramage was believed to smoke an ounce
nd chew an ounce daily. Old Bill Tervet at Pit 1, who was a Carlisle
ative and saw to the rebuilding of all the Drummond 'Jumbos' or
–6–0 engines, was reputed to chew and spit so much that the
ompany was considering floating the rebuilds out instead of carrying
em out with the crane!

From Drummond's day down to the end of the Caley's independence
here were only three valve setters at St. Rollox. The most senior was
rthur Hovill, who retired about 1916. Arthur had a box for holding
is trammels and other gear which was beautifully painted and lined in
he correct Caledonian colours with the crest on the lid. There was also
plate with 'Arthur Hovill F.R.S.V.S.' inscribed on it – the latter being
Royal Society of Valve Setters'. Another remarkable employee who
as been mentioned was Dunky Turner who repaired nothing but 'pug-
ies' (0-4-0s) and came to know each one individually – when the cylin-
ers were altered about 1910, a thicker flange was put on the steam
hest, thus requiring a larger hole in the main frame. Somehow the
rawing office never got around to issuing a new drawing for this modi-
ication. Much later, when one of the pugs was being given a new
ylinder by Watty Cookson, Dunky could recite the size to make the
ole from memory, although it was nearly a decade since such a cylin-
er had been renewed!

The Caley men had a thirst for knowledge and an enthusiasm for
videning their horizons. This of course brings us back to the business
f "getting eggsperience". John Jackson, who shared the work on the
ig engines at Pit 17, told me about how this was accomplished in the
890s. About twice a year or so, several lads whose 'time wis oot'
vould get together and arrange to go to England in search of 'eggsperi-
nce'. In those days there was a silver band in Springburn. A four-in-
and brake would be hired and left the Balgray with the lads aboard
nd with the band in front. The procession was thus escorted down
Castle Street, where the brake set off for the Central or St. Enoch sta-

tions. Once South of the Border, the new journeymen went to various railway works, or to private locomotive builders. As John Jackson said 'Your lines from Springburn got you a job in any of them'. After some eighteen months absence, in which they might serve in a dozen establishments, the lads would return to Springburn, look around for an opening and choose where to throw in their lot, usually for keeps.

No wonder Springburn craftsmen were proud of their heritage; their fame spread not only to England but also abroad, for many left their homeland to serve on railways all over the world. And most youngsters who came into the works were happy to learn from these good workmen who were willing teachers to all who showed a genuine interest and it was in their footsteps that I was determined to follow.

Caley apprentices were of various types and backgrounds. There were the disinterested and frankly dull who had drifted into the work and simply frittered their time away; when it was complete they were out on their necks. I was different, as I had the engine 'bug', and because I always pestered the older men and chargehands for answers to my thousands of questions, I was marked out early as 'one who wanted to get on', and much help and attention thus came my way.

The Caley followed the London & North Western Railway in many of its practices, and it took pupil apprentices. There were two categories of these lads. Firstly there were those who went to the University in the winter, and spent the summer at St. Rollox or elsewhere. They usually were about three months in each department, moving around within it to get a general idea of the work. They then completed their time by spending six to eight months in the drawing office and also did some firing on the footplate. When their apprenticeship was over, most of these fellows went overseas, to Canada, to Argentina or elsewhere, taking their expertise with them. The other kind of pupil was the eager beaver who went three or four nights a week to the 'Tech', as it was called then. They served the normal apprenticeship, except for a final year at St. Rollox, which was again spent in the drawing office. Many of these became technical assistants or graduated to being shed foremen. The day of the experienced driver rising to the position of senior foreman at a running shed was passing and, while a driver could still become the shift or running foreman, the number one spot was increasingly reserved for the man with superior mechanical knowledge. These pupils were often eyed with suspicion by the men on the shop floor, but then some pupil apprentices swaggered about and were rather condescending, which did not go down well with the old hands.

At pit 18 there were but two apprentices, myself and a lad who was older than I, and whose main function was simply to run messages, especially outside – there were ways and means of getting out of the works during working hours. So George went to the bookie, smuggled in beer, went for 'fags', and was quite happy about it. What he learnt about locomotives is open to question, but surprisingly he was kept on when his time was in as an apprentice.

At Christmas and New Year the men at the pits would have a collection for the apprentices – this usually meant a couple of shillings a week for two or three weeks prior to the holiday, and it was given to the lads on the day the works shut down. The same custom was followed at the Glasgow Fair, but then a box was placed in the window of the store, and the men in the shop contributed some coppers to it each week.

There were also women in the employment of the Caledonian Railway at St. Rollox. They had come there before the First World War, but during that crisis, due to the shortage of manpower, their numbers were greatly increased. These 'lassies' were to be found in the carriage department working at the making of upholstery and trimmings, in the canteen, and in the offices. But the toughest of the lot took care of the sewing for the boiler claddings. Men were forbidden to go near their work room, but in my opinion a look at its occupants was more than a sufficient deterrent.

After about 14 months at pit 18, Harry Rennie summoned me across to his little desk one afternoon, and said, "I've spoken to Mr. Hallam (who was the Chief Foreman), and if ye want to learn how tae read a drawin' ye'd better get intae the template shop. As Harry put it, "If ye can read a Caley drawin' ye can read yin anywhere!". So I moved off to the template shop, which opened up new horizons for me. And I certainly picked up the art of reading drawings.

# CHAPTER THREE

## An Improver's Lot

THE CHARGE HAND in the Template Shop was 'Young John' Harrower, a son of the outdoor manager. John was a bit of an aristocrat, even a fop, with a taste for opera. In fact he was a member of an amateur operatic society, and we were often regaled with selections from Il Trovatore and the like. He very much relied on his journeyman, Bob Hood, who saw to it that the shop work was efficiently carried through. Bob was a comic, and he would entertain us with 'Horsey keep your tail up', or 'It ain't gonna rain no more', or other popular ditties of the day whenever he saw John coming – much to the latter's disgust. Bob could remember all the details of every class of Caledonian engine, and I was amazed at how he could rattle off the particulars without any trouble at all.

I soon realised that 'Young John' was a bit of a layabout; he used to march around with a drawing rolled up under his arm, and walk through the various shops, chatting to anyone who would take time off with him. But there was a sharp wee gaffer in the boring shop and one day he asked John what the drawing was for. John hadn't a clue, and had to roll it out to see what it was – to the vast amusement of the bystanders!

The template shop was an education. My biggest job there was having to make the motion templates for the 956 class, which had both Walschaerts and a derived valve gear. From the working drawing, the template was all marked out on sheet steel. After that it was punched out in the boiler shop, and then filed up carefully to its finished size. These templates were then used for machining the various parts for the actual gears. Our daily work mostly consisted of marking off material for either drilling or machining, plus taking details from drawings in order to make sheet metal templates – and we were always kept busy. A typical day in the template shop would find Bob Hood and me working on patch plates for locomotive frames; then out in the yard we would mark off say five sets of frames for rebuilds. Back in the machine shop we would prepare 20 to 25 gusset stays for frames for the drilling machine. I recall that once we went up to the North British Locomotive Company's works at Hydepark to borrow their flanging blocks for marking the firebox plates for the 956 class.

As a member of the template team I found I also had a roving commission to visit nearly all the departments in St. Rollox. Quite often my jobs took me to the boiler shop but it was the one place where I detested having to work. First and foremost the foreman there was a roaring bully of a man who cursed everyone about the place. I soon discovered, however, that all boilermakers seemed to be more or less of the same type – rough, aggressive fellows with a complement of pretty desperate oaths. They were all on piece work so they persistently harried us to distraction if we were marking anything off for them. I was frightened of them at first but Bob Hood could hold his own with them, and so the more they bawled the longer we took. The din in the place was terrific, and most suffered from some degree of 'boilermaker's deafness', as the complaint was called. It was always a relief to escape into the boiler mounting shop, where some semblance of calm prevailed and Harry Clow, the chargehand, could always produce the teapot.

The grades in the boiler shop would have puzzled an outsider. There were platers, tubers, stayers, borers, tappers, holder-uppers, and holder-oners; there were riveters and rivet boys – believe it or not, some of these fellows were over 50 years of age. I loved to watch them heating the rivets in their little fires. When the rivets reached the right colour, the rivet boys would seize them with tongs; then they would throw one perhaps ten feet with a deft flick of the wrist to the holder-on. He caught it in a scoop, grabbed it with another set of tongs, and shoved it into the hole, hammering it home with his heavy holding-on hammer. Then the two riveters would get on to the job, hammering up the rivet with their hammers as a snap head or flat as required. This expertise has been lost with pneumatic rivetting, and it was a skill which could be seen in every engineering works in Glasgow.

At St. Rollox the cylinder shop was smallish, and separate from the main machine shop. Once the cylinders had been machined and bored out, they were taken into the cylinder shop for fitting. All the Caledonian locomotives since the 1882 Oban bogies had inside cylinders, and the making of these required special techniques. Inside cylinders were cast in two halves and the joint between had to be absolutely steam tight. This was effected by setting up each half with the centre joint on top; one half was then faced up by means of a huge surface plate lightly coated with 'red marking', a fine ochre mixed with engine oil. The fitter examined the markings and reduced the heavily marked portions by means of scrapers; this went on until he had a perfect face on the casting. The next stage was to set the first half up in a cradle upside down, where the finished face was smeared with the marking and then lowered on to the other half. A shaft with a crank that was coupled to the cradle pushed it to and fro to mark the undressed half. The cradle was then lifted and the second half was faced up. When both halves were to the chargehand's satisfaction they were jointed with boiled linseed oil; fitted bolts were driven into place and the nuts tightened by machine. Meantime the valve and cylinder cover faces were prepared by the apprentices in the shop again by means of a surface plate.

The wagon shop never interested me; the men there were all on piece work and went at their jobs hell for leather all the time. The carriage shop was quite different, and real craftsmanship was displayed in the superlative coach building which was done there. The paint shop was truly fascinating – being calm and peaceful after the incessant noise in other parts of the works. Things were so quiet that one could converse with a fellow workman two carriages away. The craftsmanship was of a very high standard; there were no spraying machines, all painting being done by hand with a brush. No wonder the carriages only required repainting about every seven years. In charge was James Jeffrey a master craftsman who became a Glasgow baillie. To see him lining out locomotive splashers free hand was really an incredible display of skill.

It was not all work, however, at St. Rollox. There were some remarkable traditions and customs in the shops. At Glasgow Fair, the second fortnight in July, St. Rollox closed down on Fair Friday at 12 noon. During that forenoon little or no work was done in the erecting shop, and the foremen kept out of the way. Shortly before midday, pay boxes rather like sentry boxes with a window at the front were set up in the yard near the gate. The pay clerks were ensconced in these, and each section had its own box. The wages were given out to the men made up in little round tin containers with the man's number on top. But do not get the wrong idea – the works did not close for holidays as we know them today, and we had to face either ten or fourteen days *without* any pay. For a few days before Fair Friday certain of the men would be keeping an eye on the foreman millwright, who was responsible for works maintenance, in order to be selected to 'work the Fair', which meant a full pay packet! And who could blame them?

But Hogmanay was different; this was the last day of the old year. For many years work went on until 5 p.m. if it was a week day or to 12 noon if Hogmanay was a Saturday, but the general observance throughout the works commenced with the start in the morning. In the erecting shop all the men to arrive by 6 a.m. would take a hammer and station themselves beside a steel plate or tank, and when the first of the 'quarter pasts' arrived he was greeted with a furious clangour of hammering – each successive arrival got a similar welcome. This performance was known as 'skitterie winter'. But the most uproarious reception awaited the chap who was the last of the 'half hours'. He was the one who had the title 'skitterie winter' for himself, and he was carried shoulder high round the whole shop while the din was ear racking; even the foremen would condescend to group themselves at their office door, which was at a higher level than the shop floor, to see who it was. There were some fellows who would have hung around outside to try to be the last but a scout was always posted at the check board to see who really was the last arrival and to escort him to the shop. Not much work was done that forenoon, and after dinner time a stage was rigged up near the new engine pits. Soon a shop concert was in progress, and somehow a few bottles had been smuggled in for a dram. While some lads would sit down to a game of cards, most of us sat round the stage either to applaud or hoot at the bold performers. And many of them were quite good, because these were the days of homespun entertainment when most could sing or play a musical instrument. Never a foreman was to be seen as they chose to reach their office by a roundabout way. These scenes were repeated in all the shops, and the cognoscenti strolled round and spotted talent in other departments.

At 5 p.m. there was a rush to get out, and soon Sherry's Bar and other Springburn pubs were thronged. If any of the younger men were being married, a dummy made up to represent him was hung up for several days near where he worked with a large notice proclaiming the dismal news. Unless he was slick at getting away he had to run the gauntlet of the whole shop on his last turn on duty before the wedding.

After my stint in the template shop, I was shifted back into the Erecting Shop to work with Watty Cookson's squad at Pit 10. I was rather disappointed with this assignment, as the highlight of working in the erecting shop was to go to the new engine pits. Many applied for the work on the new locomotives but few were chosen – as one of the old hands said, "You either had to get a reference from a kirk elder or a publican – preferably the latter!" For many years Willie Forsyth was the chargehand there – he built all the new Caley engines from 1900 until about 1911, when he became foreman. Most of the chargehands in the shop were selected from these new engine pits, and their names were always linked with the fine Caledonian locomotives which they had helped to build. Will Grant was in command of the construction of new engines in my day. He was a former Great North of Scotland Railway man who had come south from Inverurie with William Pickersgill and there was some heart-burning in the Erecting Shop about his preferment. But Willie knew his book, as he had been for some years at Hydepark with the North British Locomotive Company. His principal assistant was well-named Willie Frame for it was a joy to watch Willie lining up locomotive frames!

Watty Cookson's pit held no excitement for me. He had three 0–6–0 tanks in the pit, all minus their boilers, having firebox renewals. So our squad was split up, and sent here and there about the erecting shop to assist the others. It usually meant being faced with such tasks as stripping down bogies, fitting axle boxes, or routine chores like that – filthy jobs most of them – and our team became adept at keeping out of the way.

Early in 1920 a steaming shed had been constructed in the yard just outside the erecting shop. Bill Crooks from Carlisle, who had running shed experience, was put in charge of it. He thus became responsible for trial runs and for seeing that every locomotive was in working order when it was sent home. Bill was partnered by Johnny Mulholland, the brake man who saw to the Westinghouse and vacuum brakes. After a week or two this pair wanted a lad with them, and due to the fact that Bill Crooks had come to befriend me – I had always pestered him with questions galore – he asked for me to be sent along to the new steaming shed. When Bill came to speak to me about it, I said, 'You bet'. I was to discover that the locomotive in steam is a completely different proposition from the cold imponderable mass of metal that it is in the shops. Get it into steam and what a transformation takes place – it becomes alive. With this a new and exciting world opens, where the steam locomotive becomes a prime mover. From this moment of enlightenment the work of the shops could never satisfy me again, and in due course I was determined to go to the running sheds.

Bill Crooks was imperturbable and very capable. We always had plenty of work on our hands. There would often be two or three engines to go on trial, and hence there was frequently overtime for us. Even when the works was on short time (the work force did not come out on Saturday in these circumstances) the steam shed men were always on the job. Before the Glasgow Fair we even worked on Sundays, as the surge in traffic at that time would bring almost every locomotive into service.

Johnny Mulholland was an enthusiast for the Westinghouse brake; what he knew about its virtues and vices would have filled volumes. He knew every trick to make it work correctly – some of these were unconventional, and authority frowned on them, but that did not worry Johnny – if the brake was okay that was all that mattered! After going through the works, most engines required to have their steam pressure reset; the mechanical oil feeds had to have adjustment while the gauge cocks had to be tested and a certificate signed to comply with Caley regulations. Then either Bill Crooks or the brakeman went with the locomotive on trial, making any final adjustments that were thought essential. So work at the steam shed was no sinecure for them but was always full of interest.

There were two teams of trial drivers at St. Rollox who had firemen that were 'accommodated', that is, on account of failing eyesight jobs had been found for them at the works. The drivers first had to resiphon the oil cups on every engine, much of their time being taken up in making 'plug' and 'tail' siphons in the lubricating systems and placing these in their correct positions. Woollen yarn was used to make little 'wicks' which were placed in the oil cups – too many strands and the oil would not flow freely, too few, and the oil ran too fast. Our drivers had a rule of thumb method for making them, but they well knew that when the engine went to its home shed its own driver would redo the lot to his own satisfaction! When the engine reached this stage it was taken from the steam shed into the yard and coupled up to its tender. Now it was time for the driver and his mate to fill the tank and the boiler and to raise steam. Then Bill would set the safety valves to pressure, while the driver saw to the preliminary oiling of the locomotive.

It was soon time to go on trial. I was often on the footplate with Bill on these outings, and although we were just 'on the job', I always experienced the thrill of being on a locomotive in steam, moving and alive. The engine would set off – rather gingerly – for Balornock shed for coaling, from where it would run out east to Kilgarth Coup (a rather insalubrious locality) on the Gartcosh Junction – Coatbridge line, where in a loop it could be carefully examined for heating, or any other faults; these might be give attention there and then at Kilgarth Coup or on return to the works. Usually two runs out to Gartcosh sufficed. Once the trials were over and pronounced sucessful, the engine's home depot was advised and would send a set of men to take the locomotive 'home' for a running-in period in its own area. Careful nursing during this phase would stand it in good stead through the coming years.

Work at the steam shed was rather unpredictable in a way. Some types of engine could be taken apart and put together again with few problems. Little or nothing would be found the matter – at least until the locomotive went back to its home depot and then its own crew discovered all the weak spots! The Caley was very much a 'one driver, one engine' railway; hence these men were quick to report any defects, and we soon heard about it! But St. Rollox always had a good name for its locomotive repairs, and even into B.R. days it continued to maintain one of the top records in the country for the excellence of the workmanship from its repair shops.

While the initial steaming was in progress, Bill kept a careful eye on the engine as steam was raised. Fitters from the repair bay where the locomotive had been serviced were 'on call' to nip any trouble in the bud, for once 20 or 30 lbs of steam pressure was introduced, weaknesses in pipes would be pinpointed and all manner of unsuspected troubles might appear. Meantime, of course, Bill, helped by me, saw to all the minor snags. This was always a time of worrying responsibility for Bill, but generally after our trial runs he could pronounce himself satisfied and then we could all relax again.

Certain engines had an unenviable name for being troublesome at the steam shed. For example the Caley's condenser fitted tanks were heartily detested, yet apart from the condenser fittings, these engines were identical to the favourite McIntosh standard 0–6–0T locomotives. Another unpopular bunch were all engines with outside cylinders – this was hardly surprising as the Company since 1882 had been an 'inside cylinder' line, but then in 1916 William Pickersgill rang down the curtain on this era and according to Bill, a lot of our problems began! It came as no surprise to find that the steam shed staff were unimpressed by the 60 class 4–6–0s of 1916 or for that matter of the 956 class when these came on the scene in 1921.

In contrast to the outside cylinder engines, the 40 class 4–4–0s, to take just one example, were welcome visitors. Once these locomotives had been through St. Rollox they could be expected to remain in service for three or four years. Prior to 1914 the coupling rod bushes, as well as the large and small end brasses of the connecting rods, were made of a type of phosphor bronze; this material had excellent wearing properties, and since a very high grade of engine oil, bought from the Vacuum Oil Company, was used on passenger engines, little or no trouble was experienced with heating brasses. It was usual for the brasses to be stripped only once between shopping dates. Axle box wear was also negligible, and what were termed 'knocking boxes' were rare.

Although the 40 class had originally been fitted with Schmidt wide piston valve rings, after a lengthy period of running, some 'ovality' took place in the valve chest liners that called for the renewal of both liner and ring. When narrow-ringed piston valves were introduced at a later date, liner trouble disappeared – to the relief of the running shed men. Heavy oil carbonisation was a problem in the early days of superheating, but it may have been due to over-generous setting of the oil feeds; finer settings gave better results. Around 1914, trouble was experienced with leaking superheater flue tubes on engines employed on the through workings from Aberdeen to Carlisle. The cause was not actually discovered but the drivers did claim it was due to bad water!

By now I could claim the title of an 'improver' – a term applied to third year apprentices and their seniors; my wages had risen from the meagre 17s.6d. a week which I earned in my first years at St. Rollox to 57s.6d, a measure of growing experience and capability as well as to the addition of war bonus payments. I felt that I had laid the foundations for a worthwile working life. Fired by Bill Crook's tales of Kingmoor shed, I resolved to move over to the running side and share in the adventures of live steam locomotives – this was to be my new challenge.

At first my enquiries about a transfer drew a blank, but one day a conversation with a driver from Balornock elicited the information that an apprentice at that shed was keen to work in the shops. He had been told that he must arrange a 'swop' with someone already at St. Rollox. Here was a rare opportunity – so off I went to Balornock to see the lad in question and to meet the shed foreman. Then it was hotfoot back to Mr. Kempt's office at the works. "Well, WHAT do YOU want now?" were his first words. I explained what I would like to do. His only comment was "You seem to know what you *do* want but whether you'll like it or not will be your affair". Within a week I was transferred and became a running shed man out at Balornock – and believe me in Caley days Balornock with its ninety locomotives was a really top link shed in which to work.

# CHAPTER FOUR

## *Balornock*

M Y ARRIVAL AT Balornock shed soon got me to revise a lot of my notions about locomotive practice. First of all I had to fit myself into an entirely new pattern of working.

There was no actual supervision as in St. Rollox works; there were foremen and chargehand fitters but you were given a job to complete and then you had to get on with it and the older chaps might not come near you. You alone were responsible, and if the engine was to be on the road at say 4 p.m. it just had to be finished by that time, and thus you had a method of supervision that was more effective than any foreman!

My first mate at Balornock was Jock McLean, whose great lesson to me was simple: "Use your bloomin' head!" Jock always impressed one with the fact that in running repairs there were no hard and fast rules. Each job, even if it was similar to one before, had to be examined on its merits. Furthermore improvisation had to be used to an extent unknown in the works where all manner of equipment and expertise was to hand. One had to become accustomed to heat, to filth, to working in cramped conditions, as well as against the clock. But the satisfaction from achievement was far more rewarding than doing a task in the works, and of course the conversations with the drivers as to the performance of the engines threw a new light on my role as a locomotive fitter.

Balornock had been opened about 1915: previously there had been an old shed near St. Rollox close to a signal box (long since gone) that was named 'Locomotive Shed Junction'; this was almost opposite the present paint shop. By the time I came to St. Rollox the old signalbox was still in use but the 'Old Sheds' as they were known were just engine stores for locomotives awaiting the works or withdrawal, or for spare boilers on flatrol wagons.

There was a story about the opening of Balornock. The old shed was to shut on a Saturday: so all the locomotives were taken over to the new shed on the Sunday, except those commencing work between 12.01 a.m. and 6.30 a.m. on Monday morning. These left the old shed on the Monday. Matters were so arranged that the first engine out of the new shed at 6.45 a.m. was none other than the star of Balornock – No. 50 *Sir James Thompson*. It was driven by George Mackie, whose regular locomotive this massive 4–6–0 was at that time. This was all very much part of being with the Caledonian Railway which had great traditions to maintain.

There were also apprentices at Balornock. Some of the Caley's apprentices came from the Empire – one of these was M. L. Mitter, who was longing to return to India to set up his own home there. He was to rise to prominence as Chief Mechanical Engineer of the State Railways in that country. He was wont to say that there was one thing his years with the Caley had taught him – that was how to make putty joints! These were common for blastpipes or steam pipes for example – as always practice makes perfect!

In my time Balornock men and their engines ran north to Aberdeen, east to Perth, Dundee and Forfar, and south to Carlisle and Lockerbie with goods trains, while the passenger workings encompassed Perth, Dundee, Crieff, Stirling and latterly Oban. Then there were plenty of local runs as well. The drivers each had their own locomotives, and these were kept and maintained in excellent condition.

The first fellows I encountered at Balornock were the cleaners. Passenger engines which were worked in the Caledonian Railway on the 'one engine, one man' principle each had a cleaner allotted to them; he had to come on duty about eight hours before a locomotive was to leave the shed. There was keen competition among the youngsters who were recruited as cleaners (as the first step to greater things) to turn out gleaming engines. Engine cleaning on the Caley was always of a very high standard.

The tools which the cleaners had were very simple – scrapers which were formed from pieces of flat bar iron hammered out by the black-smith to form a tool for scraping dirt off the engine, and plenty of waste from rags. The actual cleaning substance was a residual type of oil which in many parts of Scotland was known as 'dook'. This was rubbed over the paintwork of the boiler, tank sides, footplating and splashers and was then polished off.

At one time, the smoke boxes were done with tallow, but latterly a concoction based on cylinder oil was used and this was polished until it shone. On Caledonian locomotives, especially passenger ones, the 'smokestack black', as it was termed, was capable of taking on an amazing lustre. Meanwhile the wheels and motion were washed with paraffin and thoroughly cleaned, while the red paint on the inside framing was similarly treated.

It was impossible for one cleaner in a single eight hour shift to give the entire engine this treatment and so a system was followed – first all the locomotive's paintwork would be completely cleaned with 'dook', while the tender would just be 'dry rubbed'; the wheels and motion, however, were thoroughly gone over every day, as was the smokebox. On the following shift, the cleaner would reverse the performance – the tender was then wiped down while the boiler would be 'dry rubbed'. And so it was feasible to keep the whole engine spotless.

There were also squad cleaners – juniors who had not yet been given an engine of their own to look after. At Caley sheds, these gangs of cleaners were given titles to show the kinds of work for which they were responsible. Some of these I recall – the 'bogie squad' which cared for passenger engines, the 'fancy boiler squad', which specialised in nothing but boilers, tank and tender sides, and the 'greasy squad' which was an apt name for the lads in one of the motion cleaning gangs.

It was also quite customary for the crew of an engine working say from Aberdeen to Perth to take the trouble to wipe over the paintwork if the weather was fine before returning. The cab was the fireman's prerogative, and he saw to the cleaning of the roof and sides, he put blacking on the firebox, and polished the brasswork, which was all part of the good housekeeping of our Caley locomotives.

When I first went to Balornock, the Caley still maintained their 'one man, one engine' system, a policy which was followed for a year or two once LMS control took over. At Balornock the top link consisted of three engines with three regular drivers: Nos. 956 James Grassie; 60 George Mackie; 50 Will Munro. They worked in turn the 7.15 a.m. to Dundee; the 5.00 p.m. to Perth; and the 7.47 a.m. to Perth, returning with the 11.30 a.m. from Dundee and the 7.50 p.m. Up Grampian Corridor which ran into the Central station instead of Buchanan Street.

A G.N.S.R. 'Subbie' hustles along the Aberdeen – Culter line, circa 1921. These suburban services were withdrawn by the L.N.E.R. in 1938. The engine is No. 90 which was Neilson-built in 1893 and had a characteristic dome safety valve.                                    [A. E. Glen Collection]

"Aul' Benachie" was a G.N.S.R. Class F 4–4–0 which came from Inverurie works in 1921, and was in service until 1955. Here, as No. 6846 in L.N.E.R. colours, the engine is seen at Elgin shed.          [A. E. Glen Collection]

*This McIntosh Standard 0–4–4T (No. 421) of the Caledonian Railway, which had come fresh from the shops, awaits adjustment in the yard at St Rollox in 1920. Built by the Caley in 1909, this locomotive ran until 1955. A. G. Dunbar is in the cab.* [A. E. Glen]

*A Monday morning at St. Rollox in 1921 finds apprentices investigating a new locomotive, No. 87, a Pickersgill 4–4–0 that had just arrived from Armstrong Whitworth & Company; A. G. Dunbar is on the right.* [A. E. Glen]

The train engine took the Grampian coaches right into the Central: the engine then followed the coaches out to Rutherglen Junction where it again took over, returning to Buchanan Street station via what was know as the "Switchback" or in other words the line via Parkhead, Kennyhill and Balornock Junction now closed. No. 50 on the 7.47 which was a "slow" returned with a van train from Perth.

The locomotives in the top link were a remarkable trio, the best known of which was No. 50 *Sir James Thompson* (to which there has already been reference). No. 60 was one of William Pickersgill's 4–6–0s of 1916, a successful though simple type of engine. In contrast, No. 956 was revolutionary, at least for the Caley. James Grassie was able to work Pickersgill's giant, making it really go. George Mackie on No. 60 was a great engineman in a classic sense, his mates agreeing that he was 'the best', an honour rarely bestowed among enginemen.

There were plenty of stories about the 956 class. In 1920 the St. Rollox works of the Caley began work on order Y 125. What were the locomotives to be? Another batch of 4–6–2 tanks, three-cylinder compounds, or a Pacific this time? Soon the initial work was in progress, and it was then seen that the engines were massive three-cylinder simples with a hint of the Highland River class about them. The 956 class as it came to be known, were built at the 'New Engine Pits' by charge erector Willie Grant, with four fitters and two apprentices to assist him.

Once the main frames were set up, with the cross staying in position some head-shaking took place – the look of the engine at that stage was so unusual! Even when the outer cylinders, the inner cylinder and the smokebox saddle were in place, some doubts were expressed about the possibility of the locomotive actually running! As construction continued, the shop was a popular place at the lunch hour – after all this was the first multi-cylinder engine built for a Scottish line for many years. (The only other one was a rather effete four-cylinder 4–4–0 for the Glasgow & South Western Railway in 1911; it never amounted to much until rebuilt in 1922). Everyone knew that the new Caley class would have the honour of being the biggest locomotives in Scotland, but handsome is as handsome does, as events were to show.

The boilers were built at St. Rollox but, as they were so immense, flanging blocks had to be got from the North British Locomotive Company as the Caley's were too small. There were three boiler rings, the largest of which was 5ft. 9 in. Once testing was complete, boiler pressure was set at 180 lbs per square inch, which may well have been a cause of the poor performance of the locomotives.

The three cylinders (18½ by 26 in.) were put in line over the bogie centre each with 8 in. piston valves. Walschaerts valve gear controlled the outside members, while a rather ingenious system of derived gear was to operate the inner valve. At this point it can be said that this combination of low boiler pressure plus the curious gearing was partly responsible for the lack of success of these locomotives. Only four were completed, and these went into service as follows: No. 956 to Balornock in the charge of driver James Grassie; Nos. 957 and 958 to Kingmoor Carlisle; while No. 959 went to Perth to work for driver George Newlands. It was normal Caley practice to allocate new engines to the senior men.

From Balornock, No. 956 ran in shop grey paint for some months with indicator shelters on the smokebox. There were quite a number of test runs in varying circumstances but nothing was published about the results. A technical inspector who took part in several of these runs thought that "the indicator results were the most curious ever seen". His opinion was that even if the Caley had continued into the 1930s no further 956s would have been built in that form.

First there was trouble with steaming. One of my notebooks shows that No. 956 was having the blast pipe reset twice in September 1922; then on three other occasions the blast pipe mouth piece was reset, the latter resetting being a ferrule (known to the men as a 'viril') inserted to reduce its original size. The firemen had problems with a grate of 28 sq. ft. Grassie's regular fireman told me that Jimmie had to work the door for him when he was firing the front of the box.

Keeping up steam in a locomotive entails much skill. It is not simply a case of shovelling in coal – it must be put where it is wanted, meanwhile one is working on a rocking, swaying footplate, where keeping one's balance is another problem. Many firemen of my acquaintance spoke of the 'imponderables' that arose. These usually came quickly, and could prove really troublesome unless the fireman knew his job.

One Sunday, Grassie took No. 956 on a test run on the 10 a.m. Glasgow–Aberdeen express, following the usual timings and stops to fit a 4-hour schedule. No. 956 behaved quite well until after Forfar when she began to go back in steam. The fireman was sure this was the result of a choked ashpan – it was too shallow. Coming home all went well. On another test train, however, as Jimmy put it, there was "mair trouble in an oor than I thocht possible".

At Carlisle Nos. 957 and 958 were having so many failures that little work came their way. The principal weakness with the valve gear lay in the valve spindle guides which were mounted on each external slide bar; stresses were set up so that these often broke until made of cast steel in place of cast iron. No. 959 at Perth ran almost continuously on the Perth–Aberdeen workings or on the Perth–Glasgow run, but its work was never superior to that which its driver George Newlands could accomplish with his previous engine, the 60 class 4-6-0 No. 64.

So unsatisfactory was the performance of the engines that eventually the valve gear was subject to alteration in April 1922 – on Nos. 957/958 Stephenson link motion was the choice for the inner cylinder, while No. 959 was given a new arrangement of the Caley valve gear with a dashpot to absorb stresses set up by the gearing. At that time No. 956 got another variation of this system which, after further alteration, became the same as that on No. 959. In the autumn of 1922, both Nos. 956/959 were again in the works to have Stephenson link motion put on the inner cylinder. This was a major mistake, as that gear has cross rods which cause the lead to decrease when the gear is notched up. Taken in conjunction with the external Walschaerts valve gear the two systems were to prove quite incompatible – the racket from the front was unbelievable! The locomotives were still ineffective giants.

Performance particulars for the 956 Class are very rare, but an examination of guards' journals for the years when the engines were on passenger rosters generally note 'time and time' overall, which shows that, in spite of their weaknesses, it was possible to coax or to thrash them along.

George Newlands' opinion was that engines similar to the River class should have been built; these he felt would have been more useful and effective. Nevertheless his conviction was that the first alteration to No. 959 was a vast improvement. If there had been intensive research into the gear problems by St. Rollox (rather than the fitting of an inner Stephenson gear), a successful engine might just have been forthcoming. James Grassie, who was to have plenty of experience of Compounds and Black Fives, thought that a locomotive like the Five should have been the choice.

When the Caley was taken over by the L.M.S., the 956 class were painted red, with the numbers 14800–14803. Latterly, in black paint, they were on main line goods trains, but were all away by 1935. The tenders were put on various McIntosh and Pickersgill locomotives and survived well into the 1950s.

No. 2 link consisted of five engines, Nos. 935 "Jock" Scott; 77 John Greig; 82 John Moore; 83 Jock Rough; 76 John Port. The preponderance of men called John will be noted but Greig was always called "Johnny", while Port was indignant if referred to other than "John". Moore alone answered to a nickname – "Gutty" but I never found out its origins. The first locomotive of the group was one of Pickersgill's 928 class 4-4-0s; the other four were robust 72 class 4-4-0s with superheaters. Nos. 76/77 were St. Rollox-built in 1920, whilst Nos. 82/83 came from Armstrong Whitworth in 1921. These locomotives were soon known as Pickersgill's "Ironclads" on account of their heavy construction, with 1¼ inch frames!

All the men in No. 2 link were capable enginemen but John Moore was a real enthusiast for locomotives. He would talk about them for hours – one night he came off the 6.10 p.m. roster about 1.15 a.m. just as a colleague came off a Carlisle goods. It was a lovely summer night and at 2 a.m. a driver going to the shed passed them sitting on a bridge that spanned a burn under the road from the shed "blethering" about engines. This man came back about 5.30 a.m. going to relieve men on another working and the two worthies were still seated on the parapet talking engines! Even John Moore's family were enthusiasts for the Caley. A story was told of John Moore's wife meeting fitter Jock McLean in Springburn Road and shouting to him "Man, Jock – ye made a grand job o' John's big end the other day"; Jock McLean's feelings can well be imagined!

Our No. 3 passenger link had two engines – a Caley 900 class or Dunalastair III No. 894, which was rebuilt with a superheater in 1916 and No. 934, a 928 class 4–4–0 of 1916 from the North British Locomotive Company. The trains worked were as follows: 4.15 a.m. from Glasgow Central to Stirling where it awaited the down "Postal" from Carlisle and transferred its train; then the Glasgow engine went to Crieff on the 5.40 from Stirling, returning to Glasgow with the 8.08 a.m. from Crieff which arrived at 9.45 a.m. Since the enginemen booked on at 2.15 a.m., it was one of the few workings that was "officially" relieved – others were of course "off the record". The afternoon working of the other engine was the 4.0 p.m. to Crieff, a local train from Crieff to Perth and the 7.40 from Perth to Buchanan Street. This latter was an Inverness train.

On the fourth link were three of our older McIntosh 4–4–0s, No. 891 of the 900 class of 1900, with Nos. 775 and 776 of the 766 class of 1897 – both Dunalastair IIs. No. 775 was rebuilt in 1920. All these locomotives won a name for their ease of steaming, as well as their smooth running but superheating was an improvement, especially in economising coal consumption. Their workings were rather local – they took out the 7.40 a.m. Oban train as far as Stirling, returning with coaching stock to Stepps, then by filling in their time with routine tasks such as the 12.15 p.m. "Dinner" train to Cumbernauld, or the Glenboig runs from Buchanan Street.

There was one other passenger link that was worked by two of the well known "Standard Goods", Nos. 744 and 596, which were fitted with tender cabs for the purpose of taking exchange traffic from Buchaan Street to Central Station or for jaunts out to Carluke. These locomotives were both examples of our ubiquitous 0–6–0s, belonging to the McIntosh 711 class which first came out in 1899. Several were put into blue livery, given the Westinghouse brake, then set to work on passenger trains. These engines were versatile – with their small wheels and copious boiler power they excelled on steep inclines, of which there were plenty on Scottish tracks.

The top goods link was known as the "Hielanmen" link – there sojourned the four engines of the Highland Railway, the tough River Class 4–6–0s which were bought by the Caley in 1915. Of these, No. 40 was the troublesome engine. In a journal I possess, I note that the left large end brass was remetalled and refitted every other day between October and 14 November 1922 when she was sent to the works and after examination it was discovered that the coupling rod pin had been inserted into a hole in the wheel boss that was not bored true. It was only a few thousandths out but it gave all the bother. The River class were actually the best engines that the Caley possessed and the only thing about them that drivers criticised was the Smith steam reversing gear; otherwise they were full of praise for these stalwarts. They were put exclusively on the Carlisle goods trains – two weeks on the 7.00 p.m. express to Upperby, returning after rest with an afternoon goods from Carlisle. One worked out Monday/Wednesday/Friday; the other on Tuesday/Thursday and on Saturday worked a train leaving at 10.30 p.m. for Carlisle. The engines alternated weekly and at the end of the period changed over to the 1–2 a.m. "Sweep" to Carlisle – one going out on Monday/Wednesday/Friday; the other on Sunday/Tuesday and Thursday. The "Sweep" was something of an institution – the train came to have that name because it swept up an assortment of freight traffic at any station along the route from Carstairs South.

The No. 2 goods link was served by four 179 class 4–6–0s, Nos. 180 to 183, St. Rollox-built engines of 1914–15. They ran to the furthest points in the Caley system – to Aberdeen in the North and to Carlisle in the South, working on a fortnightly rotational basis. The 179 class were superheaters; they too gave excellent performances on heavy freight trains, although they were always in blue paint. One of their runs was the 11.55 p.m. to Aberdeen, a class A express goods which ran non-stop to Blackford where the engine took water, thence through Perth General where it paused to pick up mail, before going on to Forfar. From Forfar to Craiginches in the Granite City, there was only time for one water stop at whatever point its crew chose.

There were five engines in the No. 3 link, all being 908 class 4–6–0s, Nos. 908 to 912. These were mixed-traffic engines in blue livery; they were impressive but got the name of being voracious coal eaters. Their workings again took in the furthest points on our network, but also brought in Stirling and Grangemouth, where the port gave much traffic as the Caley was the owner of the harbour there. Examples of their runs were the 1.30 p.m. "Jubilee" to Aberdeen; 8.20 to Carlisle; and the 9.0 p.m. to Stirling and Grangemouth. This latter was a weekly working to let the men have a day at home each week.

Once the LMS came on the scene the 179 class livery was black, but the 908 class which were in the same category on the Caley were given the LMS maroon passenger livery!

No. 4 goods link was served by a variety of engines of the 0–6–0 type. There was No. 300, the first of Pickersgill's 300 class 0–6–0s of 1919, plus a group of McIntosh goods engines of the 812 class of 1899. These operated in pairs on the 7.08 p.m. to Forfar; 3.20 a.m. to Locker-bie; and the 1.30 a.m. Perth. All worked in the usual fashion, a fort-night on each working, and about the middle of 1922 they took on a job to Carstairs at 5.30 a.m. – to allow the men a day shift week so as to be at home each night for a week. All those workings from Links 1 to 4 entailed booking-off away from home and yet no one seemed to object to the principle.

Following on the goods links, there was a "relief" link and this was taken by drivers and firemen who were termed "availability" men – able to go on to any of the higher category workings on account of sickness, holidays or other such interruptions. There were also the usual collection of goods mineral working and shunting assignments; the local goods workings were either "Mineral" or what were known as the "Short Roads". Examples of these were the trains to Ross Yard, Hamil-ton, to Glasgow Docks, or Motherwell, that if truth were known at times were performing little work. Some local runs, of course, kept the same engines on the roster for long enough and very often had the same driver who was an "accommodated" man. There was No. 378 for inst-ance, one of the original 'Jumbos', which was William Marr's engine: he was always known as the Earl of Mar. Another was No. 759, a 711 class 0–6–0, which was the ballast engine.

Many of these locomotives were known as pilots. Now a "pilot" in its Scottish sense was just a locomotive whose regular base was maybe a local colliery, an iron or steel works, harbour, or factory, or the rail-way's own shops. Favourite Caley engines for the light shunting jobs were the "wee puggies". For heavier haulage, the Jumbos, with the steam brake, which were in black paint with red-and-white lining, were usual.

Then we also had the passenger station pilot for Buchanan Street, an

–4–4T, No. 104 (one of the Balerno pugs of 1899), manned by relief men from 4.30 a.m. until 6.0 a.m. the regular crews working from 5–2, or 2–10; No. 104 being again worked by relief men until 12.30 a.m. So this little engine was on the job almost round the clock. These 104 class locomotives were the neatest little tanks imaginable, with 4 ft. 6 in. wheels.

When the new 4–6–0 Pickersgill Oban bogies were brought into service in 1922, six came to Balornock, and two went to Perth. They were not put on the Oban line, however, until well into 1923, on account of problems with clearances. After running-in, they went onto goods workings on the fourth link, with the 7.08 p.m. from Buchanan Street to Forfar, the 3.20 a.m. from St. Rollox to Perth – all booking-off workings. The Perth pair spent most of their time on local runs from that centre.

The 191 class was thus rarely seen on passenger workings, although one of ours sometimes took a local to Cumbernauld and back, stopping at all the stations en route, as this was a favourite 'running-in' turn for Balornock engines. If a clear photograph of these engines is examined, a support for the valve spindle will be seen on the end of the slide bars nearest the large end of the connecting rod. At first, there was much trouble because this support kept breaking off, causing the engine to fail. To correct this the support was replaced by a cast steel one which was the solution as on the 956 class.

There was also a remarkable set of shunting engines. Top of the list came No. 498, a close-coupled 0–6–0 tank, which was the first of the class. No. 498 was the "Eclipse" pilot, earning the title of the Braby pug. The reason was that this little tank locomotive spent all its time shunting at F. W. Braby's sheet metal works in Springburn, where the curvature of the lines was rather severe (the 0–4–0ST which once was active there became too light for the heavier wagon stock coming into use). Nearly forty years after, the same engine in British Railways guise was still at Balornock but was a colliery pilot, as Braby's like so many other firms was shut, the work being transferred elsewhere.

The 498 class were cumbersome engines but well suited to shunting; about 1921 the North British Locomotive Company built some similar engines (except for their saddle tanks) for collieries in South Wales. These were pure Caley, even to the smokebox wing plates. For all I know some may still be in existence. In the repair yard at St. Rollox were the 0–6–0 tanks Nos. 203 and 204 of the 29 class, built there in 1895. They once were notable for their condensing gear, but this was taken off pre 1914. A couple of similar engines were also shunters at Robroyston, where the Lambie 0–6–0ST No. 218 kept them company.

At Buchanan Street goods station there were three 0–6–0ST locomotives, Nos. 400–2; the first lot came from St. Rollox in 1887 as 232 class engines, which soon earned the title of "Jubilee pugs". There was also one veteran 0–4–2 tender engine driven by Jim Robinson who had been No. 50's first driver when it was allocated to Balornock. This 0–4–2 spent all day shunting in the "Stores" at the works and it was what could be termed a really cushy number for her crew.

Last but not least there was the famous Caley single-wheeler No. 123. This engine, which won fame in the races of 1888, was at Balornock as No. 1123. In those years the single-wheeler's principal employment was running the Officers' coach (which meant about three trips weekly), or Directors' Specials. Royal train piloting, which was once a preserve of No. 1123, was by the 1920s the responsibility of the shed working the Royal train.

To give train crews a respite, an unusual system was operated among the shunting pilots. A set of men would be given 0–6–0T No. 516 to go to Buchanan Street, there to take up the workings of various engines in turn which were to go to Balornock for coal and servicing. When they finished at the station the engine with another set of men would go to the Top Yard and the same performance would take place there – so 516 put in about 24 hours on this job and went on at it all week!

After the Grouping, I recall that quite a lot of "running-in" of engines from the works took place, but in Caledonian days this was very much frowned upon. Each shed ran in their own locomotives: for instance if No. 114 at Carlisle was to go to the works, her driver (Will Craig) brought her, and when complete he went for her. Thus drivers from Aberdeen, Oban, or even Stranraer came to the works for "their injins"; this was an arrangement that was worthwhile, as they took much interest in the maintenance of their locomotives.

The shed foreman (no shed masters or depot engineers then) was James Liddell (or the "Major" as he was usually termed), a strict disciplinarian but a very fair man; there also were three running foremen as well as two charge hand fitters – one on day shift, and one on night shift. In those days there was no change-over of shifts – this came later when the night turns were paid a night allowance and then all the staff wanted to get in on the act. To balance things up, the night men missed out on the Sunday turns which came the way of the day men about once every six weeks.

There were some stories about the fitting staff; once when No. 60 was stopped for a burst piston head there had been complaints for some time about the front cover on the superheater header always blowing out. It was discovered that the cover had a slight warp so one of the itters made a joint of sal-ammoniac and cast iron filings, or in other words a rust joint, and as the engine stood for about 15 days after it was made it had every opportunity of rusting up fully. George Mackie was quite pleased on No. 60's return to service to have no blowing joints; but when it went to the works for overhaul the fun commenced, for the cover would not come off! So they had to fit a new header. Generally the passenger engines gave little trouble – the 'one man one engine' operation cut down on snags. Much more notice was taken of small defects that were checked before they became serious.

With 90 locomotives to house, to service or to maintain at Balornock, the engines were carefully put in their places by three drivers who were known as "arrangers". Hence the locomotives came out in the correct sequence for their rosters.

Prior to 1914, the Caledonian Railway had a greater number of named trains than any other network in Britain. The company was very much aware of the value of publicity and sought imaginative ways of capturing the attention of potential travellers by rail. The Corridor and the Tourist, the Grampian Corridor or the Boat trains were particularly well known, but I soon discovered at Balornock that there were some others with unofficial titles which were unfamiliar to the public. One of these was the "Whores Express" – this was the last train from Buchanan Street station to Stirling on Saturday nights. The last train for Glenboig, on account of the insobriety of its passengers, was known as 'The Drunks' Special'!

When nearing the completion of my apprenticeship I was set to work with a labourer to help me. This was quite a step up; it meant that I had to tackle all types of work – the only difference between myself and the journeymen being that I was allowed more time for any task and naturally got less money for it! I was very much aware that one stood or fell by one's performance, as it was really a test before apprenticeship was over. Perhaps the toughest part was to acquire confidence in oneself; anyhow I sailed into every job that came my way with Jock McLean's lesson firmly in my mind – use your bloomin' head! Jock was wont to amble quietly round when I was on a tricky assignment, ostensibly to borrow a tool or share a cigarette; in the course of this he always contrived to give me some sound advice about what I was attempting. Many years after when I was in the position of having to supervise apprentices I employed a similar method, though not always with much thanks on some occasions, may I say.

I treasure a sheet of paper on which is written "Caledonian Locomotive Department".

"To whom it may concern,

This is to certify that Alan G. Dunbar completed three years and five months in St. Rollox Works, and the balance of five years in Balornock running shed as a locomotive fitter apprentice. During that time he was found to be an excellent timekeeper: attentive to his duties; and was found to be an excellent workman. He is being retained in Company's service as a journeyman fitter.

For William Pickersgill
(Locomotive Superintendent)
John G Barr

John Barr was a fair man, and a good boss, but about 1923 I foun myself on the carpet as a result of getting mixed up with the Roy. Train. Usually the West Coast route was the chosen line. First of all, royal progress by rail was quite a performance. The day before th Royal family were to set out for Balmoral, unbeknown to them I wa remaking the blast pipe joint on one of our Drummond Jumbos, Nc 542. Now this 0–6–0 was usually on a local colliery line, which was day shift job, but one of the bosses sent her out at 11.15 p.m. on "Th Newton", as it was called. This train came home to Balornock via th loop at Gartsherrie to Gartcosh Junction box. Somewhere along tha line the blast pipe joint blew out. No. 542 was steaming poorly; sh was pulling thirty wagons full of coal so she stuck on the Heather Be] crossing, snarling up the C.R. mainline to the north plus the N.B. lin to Coatbridge. What was worse, by the time the men on the spot go an engine up from Motherwell to shove No. 542 and the wagons roun the loop, the Royal Train had been held up for fully ten minutes a Coatbridge. There was panic among those in authority. When I came t Balornock the following morning I was told to go up to Mr. Barr' office at once. Mr. Barr looked grim:

"Were you on that job?"

I could only say "Aye".

"Is that all you have to say?"

I said "Really no", but what I might say would most likely not pleas him.

"Come on, out with it", was Mr. Barr's answer.

"Well", I said, "Why all the fuss? If the Royal family had any sens they would be asleep. If it were my family on the train would there b all this carry on?"

Mr. Barr began to laugh. "I agree with you, but keep that to your self. Get out now and don't let it happen again".

When the L.M.S. took over, "economy" became the watch-worc and the experts from Derby came up to look at us. After a couple o days at Balornock their recommendations principally concerned the absence of receptacles in which the staff could place greasy waste! Soon the lame chap who swept up the mess for us got the sack; so much for economy. . . .

Soon, too, strange locomotives began to appear at Balornock. About 1924 a former Midland Class 4 0–6–0 (No. 3839) was sent to Kingmoor Carlisle and put on the 8.15 p.m. goods to Glasgow Buchanan Street. This was a Kingmoor "book-off" job, being worked night about by a couple of our Caley 2–6–0s, usually Nos. 36 and 37. Billy Raphael was driving No. 37 at this time; so he was given No. 3839 plus the task of filling in a special report for the Locomotive Chief on its performance when he got back to Glasgow. Billy Raphael never wasted words. "No blooming use", was his opinion, and that is what he wrote. Of course he was put on the mat for that, but the following night was back on No. 37 again!

So as you will have seen I was to encounter a great variety of locomotive types (short of Pacifics) in my years at Balornock – everything in fact from "wee puggies" to prestigious 4–6–0s. It gave me excellent experience.

Many railway enthusiasts will remember Balornock in its L.M.S. or B.R. years. Its site is now a riot of weeds; the once-familiar noises of the place which I recall so clearly, are ceased – the pulsating Westinghouse pumps, the shrilling of jets of steam from lifting safety valves and the scrape of coal shovels on steel plates – and gone also the smell of hot oil, of grease, of steam, of sweat in the air. Yes, I remember Balornock with its ninety locomotives – it was top link.

# CHAPTER FIVE

## *The Line the Grampians Rode*

TO MANY PEOPLE in Scotland the closure of the Strathmore route from Perth to Aberdeen was a cause for regret. The line owed its development to one of last century's great engineers, Joseph Locke, whose ambition it was to build a trunk railway the length of Britain from London via Aberdeen to Inverness. It was a dream which he was able to fulfil only in part, although he was the engineer responsible for the construction of the toughest stretches from Crewe northwards into Scotland. The link from London to Crewe was the work of others. In the course of time the whole railway to Aberdeen was to achieve fame as the West Coast route and for over a century linked the two major urban centres at the extremes of this isle.

The enquirer may well ask why the principal route from Carlisle and Glasgow to Aberdeen was closed. The answer is found in that overrated word 'viability'. The line at present in use involves running extra miles from Perth to Dundee, through the bottleneck of Tay Bridge station, then a circuitous journey along the coast to Kinnaber Junction where the former Caledonian Railway route is met. The whole hinterland of Strathmore, with its rural centres of Coupar Angus, Brechin and Forfar, now has to suffer (as far as passenger traffic is concerned) a railwayless existence.

To railway enthusiasts the Strathmore line was a favourite – it traversed rolling countryside with wide vistas to the distant hills; as far as locomotive running was concerned there was always the possibility of exciting happenings. The line was a tough road in some respects. On leaving Perth there was a stiff pull away to Stanley Junction seven miles out. After passing Ballathie box there was a dip to the crossing of the Ballathie viaduct over the River Tay. From a shortish climb to Cargill the line was nearly level all the way to Forfar, where it negotiated a sharp curve through the station. An undulating section was then followed to Guthrie, where the 'Guthrie Gates' were a landmark to enginemen, who reckoned them a halfway mark between Perth and Aberdeen: 'We're halfway hame noo' was the thankful comment on many a footplate.

North of Guthrie the descent of Farnell Road bank began: the incline varied between 1 in 107 and 1 in 122 up to the dip at Bridge of Dun; from Dubton a gentle rise brought the line up to Kinnaber Junction. (The line is intact from this point to Aberdeen). From a short downhill section near Craigo, the line comes up the Marykirk bank into Laurencekirk, where a series of rising grades takes it up to Carmont; from this point the five mile long Fetteresso bank enlivened with reverse curves sweeps the line into Stonehaven. The line then climbs in stages to Portlethen but to the traveller this is perhaps the most exciting part of the journey, with breathtaking views seawards over the cliff tops to rocky stacks and storm girt bays. From Portlethen the descent into Aberdeen commences, and finally through an immense reverse curve the railway runs past Craiginches into the Granite City.

Travelling south from Aberdeen the engines faced a gruelling climb up to Portlethen which often gave plenty of trouble, especially on the curve past the Bay of Nigg towards Cove Bay, where gales sweeping inland from a tempestuous North Sea have brought trains to a standstill. Early in 1924 I caught the 5.30 p.m. from Aberdeen. On moving out on to the exposed curve past the Bay of Nigg, the train was struck head on by the furious gale which was raging. In spite of steam sanding gear, no sand would stay on the rails. The train was blown to a standstill, although we had two Caley Superheater 4–4–0s, Nos. 39 and 119, from Perth shed that day. Even with the assistance of a banking engine sent out from Aberdeen, plus the valiant efforts of the firemen in shovelling ballast on to the rails, we took 55 minutes to pass Cove Bay station. Truly, when the North Sea becomes wild, it can create troubles ashore as well as for oil installations at sea.

On the Strathmore route fast running became legendary. It may all be summed up in a place name, 'Kinnaber', which at one time must have been the only signalbox in Britain which was known all over the country. This arose from the publicity given to 'The Race to the North' which was staged between the West and East Coast railway partnerships in 1895; the results overall left the honours with the West Coast route. After the 'Race', there grew up a tradition of fast running on the Caley main line that was unequalled anywhere else in Scotland. From the time of the McIntosh 'Dunalastair' marques down to the final years of steam traction when Gresley's magnificent A4 Pacifics graced the route, superlative running was a daily occurrence. These locomotive sprints from Perth to Aberdeen and back were principally the achievement of two sheds, Perth and Ferryhill, Aberdeen. If enginemen from the Caley set the initial standards, then their successors from the L.M.S.R. and B.R. depots showed that they too were experts at the job.

The first named train to frequent that Strathmore route was the 'Tourist', which is said to have been introduced on 1 August 1869; it left Euston at about 8 p.m. to run north via Carlisle, with coaches for Perth, Aberdeen and Inverness. In the course of time on the Caley system, the 2.20 a.m. from Carlisle was always known to the staff as the 'Tourist'. Even in L.M.S. days, old servants of the company still knew the train by that name. The return 'Tourist' set out from Aberdeen about 5.40 p.m., but after some years its departure time became 7.50 p.m.

It was Irvine Kempt, the General Superintendent of the Caledonian Railway from 1871 to 1902, who first saw the potential for time-saving on the Strathmore route. It was he who introduced the famous 60 m.p.h. timings between Forfar and Perth which were to set the pattern for high speeds which continued until the closure of the route. In 1899 four trains were running from Forfar to Perth on the 60 m.p.h. basis. In that year the press announced the arrival of the Caley 900 class.

'Mr. John F. McIntosh, Locomotive Superintendent of the Caledonian Railway Company, has just turned out from the St. Rollox Works a number of new engines to which considerable attention is being given from the fact that the far famed 'Dunalastair' Class has been put in the shade by their successors, the 'Breadalbanes' (a class chosen by the Belgian government with much success for their fast Royal Mail expresses), and that these are in turn eclipsed by the new '900' class . . . meant to cope with the increasing loads of the West Coast expresses over the heavy grades of their main line'. The account continued:

'The locomotives are of the four coupled type . . . the special fittings include McIntosh's patent gauge glass protectors, steam sanding devices, steam train heating, and the Westinghouse brake. Other special

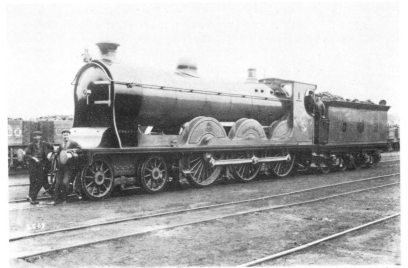

*C.R. No. 50* Sir James Thompson, *the pride of Balornock shed, was built in 1903 as a member of the 49 class; these locomotives at that time were the heaviest and most powerful in Britain.*　　　　*[A. G. Ellis Collection]*

*The Grampian Corridor Stock of the Caledonian Railway formed "a train de luxe at the ordinary fare". Here No. 60, a Balornock engine which was constructed at St. Rollox in 1916, is seen on an Aberdeen – Glasgow express near Stirling, circa 1922.*　　　　*[A. G. Ellis Collection]*

*The author beside one of his charges, a former N.B.R. 0–6–2T at Parkhead.*
*This engine was built as No. 9240 in 1925 but was modelled on the N.B.R.*

rrangements include the concealment of all pipes, brake rods etc., so as o make the locomotive look as symmetrical as possible'.

Well balanced and handsome in appearance, the 900 class or Dunalasair IIIs certainly were. Soon the new locomotives were at work on the Strathmore route. By 1906 the Caley had become renowned for its fast running, the only other British railway company approaching its expresses for sustained high speeds being the North Eastern. In 1909 the down 'Tourist' was allowed 34 minutes for the Perth–Forfar stretch, whereas the following down Postal (non-stop to Aberdeen) was only given 33 minutes for the distance of 32½ miles! The 5.30 p.m. from Aberdeen had only 32 minutes to cover the same ground.

The coaching stock on the Caledonian had to complement the refinements of its locomotives. In 1905, a writer in 'The Locomotive Magazine' noted that fifteen new carriages were under construction at St. Rollox works; these represented 'the acme of luxury yet reached for the third class traveller'. The carriages were designed for the Caley's express trains between Glasgow Buchanan Street, Stirling, Perth and Aberdeen, as well as for the Glasgow-Central to Edinburgh-Princes Street route. They were 68 ft. 6 in. long overall and ran on two six-wheeled bogies of Fox's patent pressed steel. The coaches were the first twelve-wheelers to be built by the Caley. Steel entered largely into their construction, the framing, side panels and roof bars being of that material. The trains were vestibuled throughout with side corridors.

The first class compartments, which had a generous width of 7ft. 1¼ in., were finished in polished walnut and upholstered in tapestry, while the thirds were decorated with polished mahogany and dark blue seats. The compartments were lit by Stone's system, each having 'an electrolier carrying four incandescent lamps'. Each car had lavatories 'neatly finished with tile floors and furnished with hot and cold water'. The reviewer remarked that 'altogether such a *train de luxe* at ordinary fares had not before been placed on any railway and the Caledonian deserve the patronage of the travelling public for their efforts to add to the comfort of long journeys'.

Once introduced on the Glasgow – Aberdeen route, these coaches became known as 'Grampian Corridor stock', and the trains were named the 'Grampian Corridor Expresses'. From the windows one saw the Grampian Mountains in the distance as the express traversed Strathmore.

The Grampian Corridor Express left Buchanan Street station at 10 a.m. After the engine there came a brake third and a brake composite for Dundee; then a brake composite for Inverness and Strathpeffer. There followed a brake third, another third, a Pullman coach, a composite, and a brake third – all for Aberdeen. Lastly there was a brake composite for St. Fillans which was slipped at Crieff Junction, or Gleneagles as it is now called.

The Aberdeen portion returned on the up 'Grampian Corridor' at 5.30 p.m. from Aberdeen. The morning 'Grampian Corridor' left the Granite City at 10.05 a.m. The composition of the train was as follows: – Brake third for Carlisle; brake compo for Preston; brake compo for London; brake third, compo, Pullman, brake third, all twelve wheelers for Glasgow; brake compo for Edinburgh.

The Glasgow and Edinburgh portions returned to Aberdeen as part of the 5 p.m. from Glasgow, the Edinburgh portions joining the train at Stirling.

In 1910, the Grampian Corridor Expresses were timed 34 minutes from Perth to Forfar, a tight timing for a train with such heavy coaching stock; the two north-bound trains slipped a coach at Coupar-Angus. The two corresponding up trains were both given 33 minutes from Forfar to Perth. Throughout the loads were reckoned either as 9 equal to 17 or 7 equal to 13½.

My friend J. D. Sherriff of Arbroath, accompanied by his father, used to travel daily between Forfar and Perth. Both were railway enthusiasts, and they allowed me to examine timings which they made in the pre-First War years. While these jottings are not logs as we know them today – for instance no information is given about the actual trains – the timings are interesting and show clearly that superlative locomotive working was general on the Strathmore route.

Although there is little to choose between the performances of various Caledonian locomotives on the Strathmore line, if a choice must be made then the members of the 900 class, or Dunalastair IIIs were very consistent performers. Let us look at some of the runs from these notes.

|  | No. 888 Driver John Hall | No. 890 Driver Sam Hynd |
|---|---|---|
| Forfar: | 0.00 | 0.00 |
| Alyth Junction: | 13.20 | 12.45 |
| Coupar Angus: | 18.20 | 17.45 |
| Perth: | 33.00 | 32.15 |
|  | Load: 3 eights | Load: 4 eights |
|  | 3 twelves | 1 twelve |

|  | No. 891 Driver Jim Russell | No. 889 Driver W. Webster |
|---|---|---|
| Perth: | 0.00 | 0.00 |
| Stanley Junction: | 10.45 | 10.30 |
| Coupar Angus: | 19.30 | 19.15 |
| Alyth Junction: | 23.00 | 23.30 |
| Forfar: | 34.30 | 34.15 |
|  | Load: 4 eights 2 twelves | Load: 4 twelves |

Driver Webster was known as "Aul Twal-Twall" from his habit of saying he was on the 12.12 p.m. ex Perth.

It is clear that throughout their sojourn on the Strathmore route, the Dunalastair IIIs gave an excellent account of themselves. Another series of timings reveal that other Caley locomotives were also capable of putting up a good showing on that line. The McIntosh 4–4–0 superheaters of the 139 class came out in 1910. Some time after their introduction, Mr. Sherriff was travelling to Aberdeen. At Forfar station he spoke to driver Peter Scott who had No. 132 that day, and of course he asked what the new engines could do. It was usual to run without steam down Farnell Road bank, and Mr. Sherriff slyly suggested to Peter Scott that he should try steaming down Farnell. Peter Scott said nothing but after a stop at Guthrie he came up to the carriage window and invited Mr. Sherriff on to the footplate. This he did, and as he put it, never before or since did he go down Farnell like it. Peter Scott opened up the regulator and, whereas it was customary to shut off at the level crossing north of Guthrie, he let the engine race on; by Glasterlaw the locomotive was doing a comfortable 75 m.p.h. Mr. Sherriff estimated that No. 132 reached well over the 80 mark before slowing down for the Bridge of Dun stop.

Engines of the Caley's 766 class or Dunalastair IIs also appeared on the Strathmore route, and were capable of fine running as the following extracts show:

|  | No. 724 (Driver James Mitchell) | No. 774 (Driver Sam Hynd) | No. 144 (Driver James Mitchell) |
|---|---|---|---|
| Perth | 0.00 | 0.00 | 0.00 |
| Coupar Angus | 19.25 | 19.30 | 19.00 |
| Forfar | 34.30 | 35.00 | 33.50 |
|  | Load: 4 eights 2 six wheelers | 4 eights 1 twelve | 4 eights 3 twelves |

All these drivers were Perth enginemen. Driver Mitchell in particular was an able performer with whatever type of locomotive he had, and there were no variations in his timings for a week at a time.

The Caley enginemen drove on the regulator and used the fixed cut-off as far as possible. Driving was as always a matter of experience. The regulator was opened until the characteristic staccato Caley 'bark' was heard and off they sailed. Of course there were refinements. The normal position for valve setting was to place the reversing lever at a point between the fourth and third notch from the centre both in the fore and back gear, and to set the valves at that point.

When driving on the regulator and using the fixed cut-off, the reverse had to be positioned at some pre-determined point and the regulator shifted to suit. Most drivers carried a bolt or a piece of metal which they fitted into the reversing lever selector plate; this allowed a finer adjustment between the notches, and thus varied the cut off position between the 5½th and 4th notch. When stopping it was customary for Caley engines to come into a station with a breath of steam still going into the cylinders, since this cushioned the pistons, the large and small ends, helping to prevent the setting up of 'knocks' on the ends themselves, and in the driving axle boxes.

About the summer of 1910 Mr. Sherriff senior was going to Glasgow. He chose to travel in the afternoon with the Up Postal, but on arrival at Forfar, the station master told him that the train was delayed as there was some trouble with the engine. It came in about five minutes behind schedule hauled by No. 888 from Perth shed. For years a veteran Caley 2–4–0, No. 428, which had been built in 1867, was standing pilot at Forfar. It was a rebuilt Conner engine with 6ft. 2in. coupled wheels and was driven by a local worthy, Andrew Soutar. This old engine carried the number 1590 briefly before its withdrawal in 1901.

The replacement for No. 428 was another 2–4–0 locomotive which originally had the number 590. It was similar in design, with 18 by 24 in. cylinders and 6ft. 2in. coupled wheels. In the course of its career this engine had six alterations in number (the Caley went in for this sort of ploy, one of its engines having eleven variations in number – which must be a record on any railway). Eventually, in 1901, this locomotive swopped numbers with the original No. 428 and just to complicate matters further became No. 1590 in 1910! By then it had become so much of an institution at Forfar that the staff continued to refer to it as 'aul 428'.

To revert to the failed No. 888; it was taken off, and old Andrew's engine was sent to couple on to the Postal. 'Aul 428' (or No. 1590 if you prefer) backed on to three postal vans, plus two corridor eight-wheelers for Glasgow – a load of approximately 150 tons. The train set out from Forfar at 4.50 p.m. with twelve minutes to make up. But old Andrew was to show his mettle. He let the old engine go like the wind. The result was that the train came into Perth at 5.25 p.m. – 32½ miles in 35 minutes flat. Andrew Soutar was well content: 'She's a gran' auld engine onywey', he remarked. Very shortly Andrew was given the new 0–4–4T No. 428 when it was fresh from the works, but he always claimed that it was not a patch on his old 2–4–0!

Numerous branches took off from the Strathmore route. These served the rich farmlands of the counties of Perth and Angus. One remembers the little branch trains at Alyth, Coupar Angus, Forfar, Bridge of Dun or Guthrie patiently awaiting the arrival of the main line expresses. Once on board the branch line coaches, there would be a smart journey, probably behind a Caley tank to a rural outpost. Do you remember the embarrassingly low platforms at Kirriemuir Junction, especially for the lassies who favoured tight skirts? Anyway, the ways of getting in (or out) of the coaches were a cause of much hilarity there. If it was at night, you may remember the halts at oil-lit stations, and the bustle of the local people.

The arrival or departure of a train at these places was always an event. And comment there was, for the country folk of the Mearns had their full share of curiosity and did not fail to express it. I have often heard such comments as these on wayside platforms: 'Aye, where's auld Tam aff tae the day? I see Miss Gordon's on the trot again, guid kens if she can afford it! Fat on earth has Colonel Scott got in that box? Wid he be sellin' some o' his fancy vases?' All this was not really unkind gossip but the natural interest of the local people in the activities of the whole community.

The Alyth to Newtyle line was known locally as 'The Trappie Railway'. The name is said to have been given to it by the navvies who worked on the making of that line. The Banff Arms Hotel in Alyth which was a popular 'howff' for the navvies also had a nickname – 'The Trap'. I recall hearing about the mother of a friend: she cleaned the station offices at Alyth for 19s. 6d. a week back in the 1890's, and she was able to vouch for these bynames.

There was a story, probably much exaggerated, about a runaway train at Newtyle. The trains from Dundee to Alyth and to Blairgowrie used to be split at Newtyle, which was an awkward place on a 1 in 60 incline. The engine and the front portion then moved off to go to Blairgowrie, leaving the rear portion standing at Newtyle platform. Now the official version of the tale is that the handbrake rod on the guard's van broke, releasing the handbrake and letting the coaches roll away, but the other view is that the handbrake broke when the guard tried to apply it *after* the air/vacuum brake on which they had been relying leaked off faster than usual! Be that as it may, the road was clear for Alyth and the coaches rolled away down the slope from Newtyle over the Burnmouth farm road, past Alyth Junction, over the A927, round a sharp curve to the right, over the Caley main line, under the A927, where the 'train' popped into Alyth junction station, through the points and away round to the left over a bridge, under another bridge and (oh, horrors!) over the A94 level crossing. All the hapless guard could do was to lean out blowing his whistle! The coaches then ran through Meigle station, under a bridge, across the Dean Water bridge, across the river Isla and on to the level embankment which stretched northwards along the foot of Strathmore.

The rising grade gradually checked the speed of the coaches and somewhere about Silvie they stopped – having now passed through two other accommodation crossings and Jordanstone station!

Thence the coaches ran back, down across the Isla and the Dean and with accelerating speed moved towards Meigle; near there they stopped and set off downwards again and after several runs back and fore across the valley, they eventually came to a halt on the Isla bridge.

The exasperated guard, breathless with anxiety and all his whistle-blowing, got out to reassure the passengers; one of these – an elderly woman – attacked him with her umbrella, beating him about the head for his inability to stop the train!

The traffic that arose on these branch lines reflected the pattern of rural activity. There were the 'fruit expresses' from Newtyle in the strawberry months, or the busy potato traffic in the autumn. Coupar Angus had an unusual goods yard layout to cope with the consignments of 'tatties'. At Forfar, too, the track arrangement was odd, resulting I suppose from the new line from Glamis joining up at that point with the existing Arbroath and Forfar Railway. The Forfar locomotive shed had a coaling plant but the remarkable thing about the depot there was that latterly half the engine shed was being used for storing potatoes!

Through the years after the 1923 groupings, a variety of locomotives frequented the Strathmore road. The main line echoed to the sound of Stanier Pacifics, and ubiquitous Black Fives, but on the branches former Caley engines were still to be seen. A friend recalls waiting at a bridge over the line on the Kirriemuir to Glamis road for what was rumoured to be the last steam-hauled express on the line. He was joined by a lorry driver who was curious as to why anyone should want to stand there of all places. My friend explained why he was waiting and the lorry driver chose to wait too. After this experience the driver must have thought that railway enthusiasts were clean daft, for in weeks to come numerous steam-hauled expresses kept turning up on the Strathmore line!

Very soon however, steam locomotives began to vanish from British Railways, so much so that by Easter 1960, when the engine on an Aberdeen – Perth train failed at Marykirk the Peak class D.1 *Scafell Pike* came to the rescue. The latter was very new then and was working a down goods.

In the years from 1960 to 1965 there were several rail excursions on Sundays from the Forfar area to such places as Helensburgh, Crianlarich, Killin, Dunblane and home, or to Oban or Ayr. These were an example of the initiative of local railway staff. The influence of the old counties was shown by the excursions starting at Bridge of Dun! At the commencement the outings were such a novelty that on the Sunday morning when the first excursion train got to Eassie, the level crossing gates were shut across the railway. There was a halt of about 40 minutes as someone had forgotten all about the special! He was most unpopular both with the train crew and the passengers.

Elderly 0-6-0s, however, continued to work such branches as those to Justinhaugh and Kirriemuir. There were stored locomotives mainly of C.R. and L.M.S.R. origin at Forfar. Then came the day when they were to be moved away. An observer who was present recalls the wheezy sound of the engines as they were towed from the yard on their journey south; the motions were not disconnected and the dry cylinders were puffing only dusty air.

My last steam run on the Strathmore route was in 1960 behind A4 No. 60031 *Golden Plover*. A friend who was with me on that occasion timed her at over 90 miles per hour through Cargill. I used to enjoy waiting by the line south of Stonehaven station in days past, and a sight that was always thrilling was to see the Up Postal gathering mails at speed. Latterly there would be an A4 in front, tearing across the rolling countryside, a plume of steam and smoke flowing from the chimney. Yes, poetry in motion, for steam memories are made of this.

There are plans afoot to have a steam railway in Strathmore again. The Brechin Railway Preservation Society from its base at Brechin Station proposes to reinstate the Caledonian Railway former branch line between Brechin and Bridge of Dun as a tourist attraction. Although the Brechin branch has been open only for coal and lime traffic in recent years, that route has now been closed by British Rail. All strength to the enthusiasts intent upon preserving a Caley branch line. . . .

Today the line the Grampians rode goes no further than Forfar for goods only. There is a yard at Coupar Angus as well as at Forfar, for agricultural traffic. There are coal sidings at Eassie and Burrelton. Of express passenger workings there are only recollections and photographs to recall past glories. Yes, the Strathmore route was unique, for it was part of Scotland's Premier Line.

# CHAPTER SIX

## *Beattock for Summit*

SCOTLAND HAS THE most extensive areas of high country in the British Isles, and its relief is often sharply accented. This is the result of its geological past which has left a remarkable range of rock types. The passage of glaciers and melt water some 8 000 years ago helped to shape the land as we see it today. Although there are major through valleys running north-east to south-west which have been an advantage to the railways, north-south routes have always been problematical. The Scottish coastal plains are narrow and discontinuous and so railway construction was awkward there too, often entailing building viaducts as on the old Aberdeen Railway, or the gigantic feats of engineering to span the Firths of Tay and Forth.

There are, however, places where high passes lead from one valley to another, a fact which assisted the construction of the early railways across such summits as Beattock and Drumochter. Even in the height of summer, these passes are bleak and inhospitable with few signs of habitation. The line sides were at one time bordered by long stretches of snow fencing, which showed that the storms of winter were no strangers there. Heavy snow falls lashed by strong winds into great drifts are always a hazard on the lines across these Scottish passes.

Beattock was the first high level pass to attract the attention of railway promoters. It was always a formidable climb for a locomotive, with long stretches at 1 in 75, but no-one really knows when the banking of trains from Beattock Station up to the summit ten miles away first began. There can be little doubt that it was accepted practice from the early days of the Caledonian Railway's main line, and continued for over a hundred years. Prior to this century, some curious banking engines are known to have been employed there, since according to the records these were usually old tender engines whose days on main line workings were long past.

On 29 March 1900, the first of the well-known McIntosh Standard 0-4-4 tanks was sent to Beattock, and it was followed at intervals by others of the same class. The type of motive power for assistance in banking trains up that steep ascent then took on a distinctive pattern. For over fifty years, these stalwart little engines performed their prosaic task as bankers, pushing hard at the tail of a train for 10 miles up, then running light 10 miles down, day-in, day-out. It may sound monotonous, but was banking really so?

The men who drove and fired the Caley tanks at Beattock did not think so, for there were compensations. The job was almost within sight of home, and during the intervals of waiting at either the top or the bottom of the bank, other activities could be pursued – reading the newspaper, or just having a smoke or a crack. Some of the enginemen on the banking rosters spent all their railway service at Beattock, and were quite content to be there. Occasionally a little variety might come from a week or so on the Moffat branch train, but the banking crews mostly worked on a shift basis that covered the twenty four hours for 7 days and 7 nights every week.

Banking a heavy train called for a considerable degree of skill in engine driving. Passenger trains when banked were normally scheduled to take 19 to 20 minutes to cover the journey from Beattock station to the summit. If two locomotives were on the train from Carlisle they usually went right through and it was common for the assisting engine to be detached at the summit. Goods trains were timed differently – Class A goods (again if banked) were allowed 25 to 29 minutes for the climb but very few goods trains ever went up Beattock without banking assistance.

The whole operation was smart and efficient. Both passenger and goods trains stopped at a pre-arranged point, while the banking engine ran out of a siding at Beattock South Box. The slip coupling was attached by the fireman. Then the driver of the banker gave three 'crows' on the whistle – the engine in front replying in the same manner. There followed another three blasts on the whistle from the tank at the rear, but by this time both engines had started moving and were soon hard at work on the bank itself. At the summit, when the leading engine had passed the down water column by the Summit box at 1014' above sea level, another blast on the whistle told the banker to slip the coupling and the little tank was left on the line while the train pulled away at increasing speed. The banking engines then returned down the bank, either light, or in front (yes, in front) of goods trains going down, for the goods in all probability would make a stop at Beattock station. It was common to see goods trains lying in the signal box sidings at Beattock in order to clear the road for more important trains. The goods trains always had to be propelled back into the loop siding, as facing points were disliked on the bank.

In past years, a reassuring sight at Beattock South box in mid-afternoon was the line up of five or six 0–4–4 tanks patiently awaiting the arrival of the down expresses. First the 10 a.m. from London-Euston for Glasgow and Edinburgh would appear; it was split at Carstairs. Then the Perth – Aberdeen portion would come along, to be followed by the afternoon train for Glasgow from Liverpool and Manchester. The Perth fast goods, and the afternoon goods for Grangemouth come in quick succession. A second portion of the express from London might be running, especially at holiday periods, and some Carlisle – Perth empty stock would probably work through. So the bankers were kept busy. In Edwardian days when, prior to the Twelfth of August, influxes of English were migrating to shooting boxes in the Highlands, the Caledonian's down 'Tourist' sometimes ran in eight or even ten portions, all of which had to be banked up to the summit, throwing an immense strain on the operating department.

On Beattock bank itself there were once four signal boxes: Auchencastle, Greskine, Harthope and Summit. All of these were open round the clock seven days a week. Greskine had a claim to fame that was not known outside railway circles – a trout lived in a rain water barrel there. With the introduction of improved signalling, both Auchencastle and Harthope were replaced by intermediate block signals, which left Greskine roughly half way up the bank as the sole remaining box between Beattock North and the Summit Box.

There were tales that became legendary about happenings on the bank; some were patently untrue, some plausible – like the story of the driver who carried a pail of sawdust on the footplate of the banker. The sawdust was thrown on the fire to produce a reassuring shower of sparks! Whenever the engine crew at the front looked back they could see the sparks flying out of the banker's chimney and believed that it must be doing its appointed task. (This tale has turned up at a few other localities and in each case the event probably took place there too). An effective way of telling if the banker was pushing properly was to stand on the lineside as the train went past and to look at the couplings. Were they tight or loose? If they were loose then the conclusion was that the train locomotive was doing all the work, and taking the banker up as well!

There were also stories, of course, of the train engine failing and the banking engine with herculean effort shoving the whole cavalcade up the bank on its own at a spanking 30 miles per hour!

With the advent of electric traction on the West Coast Main Line, the incline at Beattock has been transformed. As a driver put it, "They flattened the bank when it was electrified and it can be climbed in seven minutes now." All the same, wet rails can still bring an electric locomotive down from 90 to 50 miles per hour, and so Beattock can still be daunting. The Caley Standard tanks were still bustling up the bank until the mid-1950s when British Railways 2–6–4Ts came on the scene. Even today, two Class 20 shunters are based at Beattock to give assistance if required.

Although Beattock was the best-known Scottish banking location, there were also places in Central Scotland where heavy or fast trains were assisted on sections of the main line. From Motherwell up to Craigenhill, for example, it was customary for heavy trains to call for a banker. Any passenger train requiring assistance had to notify Lesmahagow Junction box ahead; in particular the up Postal was often helped along from Law Junction to Craigenhill as it had lost momentum at Law, where it stopped to attach the Glasgow portion. The locomotives assigned to banking duties on this stretch were often Caley 'Jumbos'. When the LMSR came on the scene, the authorities gave up the use of slip couplings. I remember that in the dip through Carluke, the Jumbo would be left well behind and labouring to keep in touch as the express tore away from it, but on the rise up to Braidwood the banker would catch up again.

The Dunblane bank north of Stirling was banked right up to the last years of steam. From Cornton box to Dunblane the line rises at 1 in 100 and thence at 1 in 88 to about half a mile east of Kinbuck. The down T.P.O. or West Coast Postal from Carlisle to Aberdeen had a very tight timing and always received banking assistance up to Kinbuck, often from a Caley 0–6–0 or latterly by BR 2–6–4 tanks which were stationed at Stirling. I have seen the Postal with its six vans or so and a Black Five in front race away on the level from Stirling out across the plain of the Forth. By Bridge of Allan it would be slowing up, giving an opportunity for the Jumbo, Standard Goods or tank which had been thrashing away with all its might, to catch up.

There were many other places where there was provision for banking assistance with passenger trains, such as from Haughead Junction to Ferniegair on the Cadzow bank, from Rosehall Junction to Airdrie, from Maryhill to Springburn Park, and from Kilwinning to Auchenmade. Brechin to Brechin North Junction and Stonehaven to Carmont were also locations where bank engines might work.

Away from the main lines, goods and mineral traffic in the Motherwell and Hamilton areas of Lanarkshire relied to a considerable extent on banking, this being normally left to the discretion of the staff on the spot. Bankers could often be observed on the Hamilton Junction (via Merryton) to Stonehouse and Larkhall lines. From Lesmahagow Junction to Strathaven (via Meikle Earnock) they were again a regular feature, which is not surprising as part of the route rose at 1 in 66. On the Baillieston to Rosehall (Coatbridge) line, from Mossend to Bellside Junction, or from Newton to Mossend, banking engines were constantly in action. Many heavy coal trains out of Ross Yard Hamilton got banking assistance; most of these assignments were given to Caley 0–6–0 tanks, although the 0–8–0 tanks were also utilised from Ross and Craighead yards out to Quarter, or to Alton Heights, to help long trains of empty coal wagons. Extra assistance on goods or mineral workings was also scheduled for many odd places, such as from Uddingston to Bellshill Junction or from Mossend up to Gartsherrie, where in sudden cases of difficulty the local pilot engine would be rushed to the scene to give a timely shove up the incline.

Another venue on the Caley where banking was practised was on the grade from Buchanan Street Station in Glasgow out to Robroyston. The standing start from the station itself up through the tunnel to St. Rollox at 1 in 79 was a stiff pull away for heavy trains. It was not uncommon for passenger trains to be banked up to Robroyston West, using the normal slip coupling. Goods or mineral trains on the other hand were also helped out to Robroyston by a banker, but there they halted while the banking engine was detached.

The Caledonian Railway also had substantial interests in the Dundee district, where there were steep ascents up from the shores of the Tay into the hilly hinterland of the Sidlaws. Banking was available for goods, mineral or empty coach trains journeying from Buckingham Junction to Liff, Lochee or to Fairmuir. There were some sharp grades on these routes – one short section 1 in 50, and several portions were 1 in 100. The inclines were not indicated on the lineside in any way, but at least they were shown in the Working Timetable! Most lots of wagons had to be banked up to Fairmuir yard and in Caley years the

0–8–0 tank No. 496 was engaged on that job for a lengthy part of the day, and for many a year.

For goods and mineral trains there were no less than 98 points on the Caledonian system where rear assistance was available; in most cases it would only be for a mile or two. Although piloting was less usual, freight trains could be piloted by an assisting engine from Greenhill to Cumbernauld where there was a rising grade.

The instructions about the loading of Caledonian passenger trains were very primitive. I have never come across a passenger load table; it did exist, but must have been kept well out of sight. The loads were reckoned as 7 equal to 14 or 8 equal to 15 (that is bogie stock equivalent to six wheelers).

The General Appendix to the Working Arrangements laid down that the maximum for a passenger train was to be "equal to 20½ vehicles" – these being reckoned on the basis of an ordinary bogie carriage as "equal 1½" while a twelve-wheeler was "equal 2". An instruction stipulated that if a passenger train was over the rostered weight, the Locomotive Department should be notified early so that "the Locomotive Foreman may consider whether additional locomotive power is required".

With regard to banking assistance on both Beattock and Dunblane banks, it was apparently left to the driver to decide whether this was required or not. It is, however, fair to say that most trains were banked, especially at Beattock. Jock McLeish used to mention that the load of the 'Tourist' in C.R. years before 1914 was 10 equal to 19 or 11 equal to 20½, these being made up respectively of 8 twelves equal to 16 and 2 eights equal to 3, or 8 equal to 16, plus 3 equal to 4½. If the Oban portion ran separately, the 'Tourist' would run non-stop from Carlisle to Perth and if the train was within the load for an unassisted passage up Beattock then it was a point of honour with the enginemen to go over the summit on their own!

Turning to the old North British, the most notorious and best-known bank on its whole system was the 1 in 42 incline from Queen Street station in Glasgow – a truly fiendish start for any train from a main line terminus. At one time, cable-haulage assisted train locomotives from the station up to Cowlairs. The cable only exerted a few tons of 'pull' on a train, which had to run forward while the cable was attached. The ascent then began. It was a time-wasting and cumbersome method, and for the descent into Queen Street brake trucks had to be placed in front of the train. In 1908, the N.B. had the first six 0-6-2 banking tanks built by the North British Locomotive Company, and from that time these engines took over the task of pushing trains up through the smoky dank tunnel. They were still on that job in the final years of British steam.

Another troublesome spot on the North British main line was at Inverkeithing South towards the Forth Bridge North signalbox. There is an incline there of 1 in 70 for approximately 2¼ miles through two sinuous tunnels, each with a reverse curve. It is an alignment that is formidable on any route calling itself 'main line', but the terrain is difficult there. On the East Coast Main Line, between Dunbar and Grantshouse, there were also calls for bankers. The slope averaged 1 in 200 from Dunbar to Innerwick – which was tolerable, but after that point it rose at 1 in 96 to Grantshouse and thus banking engines were available for this section. Both at Inverkeithing and at Dunbar an assisting engine was based. The favourite variety at Inverkeithing was a North British 4-4-0 of the Intermediate class, or a dual-fitted 0-6-0, while for the Dunbar – Grantshouse duty a Glen class would be sent from St. Margaret's shed. At numerous locations in Fife, banking engines were at work helping coal haulage on the short steep inclines in which that region abounds. Quite often assistance was at the front. Piloting on the North British was covered by a rigid rule – the pilot must be coupled to the train, while the train engine took the lead. The N.B.R. was the only Scottish line which insisted upon this. Banking was also common from Hawick up to Whitrope in the Borders.

Away from the east coast, North British bankers could also be found working out of Rothesay Dock in Glasgow up to Gartsherrie with iron ore trains. These either took the old Union line round Glasgow, or came through Glasgow Queen Street Low Level out to Gartsherrie. And, of course, bankers served another purpose for as well as pushing they could pull, thus assisting braking and hence they were a feature of iron ore trains which were always double coupled. For additional braking power on the North British, bankers could be seen at the rear of trains going downhill on sharp curves such as the Bull curve ('bull' to rhyme with 'mul') at Lenzie where a branch came off the old Edinburgh and Glasgow line.

On the Glasgow & South Western Railway, piloting was referred to as 'coupling'. When a heavy train was rostered, the order would be given 'a couple for the Pullman'. On the Great North of Scotland, the only instance ever observed was an 0-4-2 tank pushing a train from the docks up the Waterloo branch to Kittybrewster, but it may just have been returning to its shed. Passenger trains over a certain weight were piloted from Aberdeen to Cairnie Junction, and goods trains likewise received assistance. Any other instances of piloting on the G.N.S.R. were likely to be locomotives returning home.

When railway promotion came to the Highlands, the Grampian Mountains were initially to prove an insurmountable obstacle. There was a bill in Parliament in 1845 for a railway to link Perth and Inverness, but the scheme was rejected because of the great heights and severe engineering problems likely to be encountered on the route. The parliamentarians were discouraged by the existing state of experience about the working of severe inclines at such altitudes. Although engineers gave assurances about the viability of the proposition, caution prevailed as the line would rise at 1 in 75 for 8¼ miles near Blair Athol, and at 1 in 84 for 7⅛ miles south from the Moray Firth coast lands. Joseph Locke and his colleagues pointed out that the Caledonian Railway had won approval for a stretch of railway at 1 in 75 for 5½ miles, and for a length of 2½ miles at 1 in 80; the engineers argued that the *length* was of little significance if the locomotives had sufficient power to mount the inclines in the first place!

The question of a line through the Grampians was again mooted in 1860. Locomotive technology had so advanced by that time that there was now confidence in the project and an Act was passed in July 1861. Construction was begun at once and the new line, 104 miles long, was open for traffic on 9 September 1863 – less than two years after cutting the first turf. A new place name entered railway parlance – Drumochter (the topmost ridge), which at 1484' above sea level is the highest point on any main line railway in the British Isles. From Blair Athol to the summit, the route rises 1045' in 17 miles. Steam locomotives had to contend with sections varying between 1 in 70 and 1 in 72 for 10 miles. The descent into Bedenoch is also steep, the line falling 747' in 18 miles, the steepest portion being 1 in 80. Nor was this all. The climb to Dava Moor, whose summit topped 1046', was also hard going, with a section of 1 in 70 for 8 miles. When the line via Carrbridge (which is presently in use) was opened over Slochd Summit (1315') in 1899, its inclines were of even greater severity, the worst being the 1 in 60 slog of 10 miles out of Inverness.

In these circumstances it is scarcely surprising that locomotives hauling trains required a helping hand to climb over these passes. On the Highland Railway, however, piloting was always more popular than banking and the drivers became expert at working two different engines in tandem. A sight to delight the enthusiast was to see a 'Castle', with a 'Loch' as pilot, taking a long passenger train south from Aviemore where there was a slight rise away from the station. Wet or greasy rails could make striking together difficult – and difficult it could be even for two Black Fives in L.M.S. or B.R. times.

On the Highland Railway, piloting became the accepted practice from Aviemore up to Slochd, and between Dingwall and Raven's Rock. The latter was a long steep ascent at 1 in 60 for six miles from Fodderty Junction to the summit of the incline. Pilot engines also appeared on the Helmsdale to Forsinard road, the hardest stretch being the rise at 1 in 60 from Forsinard to the summit at the county march between Caithness and Sutherland. Trains were also piloted from Forres, up to Dunphail on the Dava line. The custom was to use any available engine to assist the train. In 1909 the first of the Peter Drummond 0–6–4 tanks came to Blair Athol to act as bankers for Drumochter. One might think that the Highland drivers would welcome locomotives specifically designed for the purpose, but on the contrary, these engines found little favour. The enginemen thought them heavy and clumsy; the water capacity was inadequate in their opinion, and what was worse, the axle boxes were always running hot! So it was with some relief that train crews saw other locomotive classes arrive at Blair Athol to act as bankers in L.M.S. years, although the same reservations were expressed about the small 2–6–2 tanks of L.M.S. provenance!

On a journey north from Perth to Inverness the best position for an observer was in the middle of the train. If weather permitted, one could

*As B.R. No. 55234, this former C.R. 0–4–4T waits at the signal box at Beattock Summit after assisting a train to the top in May 1953. The locomotive was built in 1922 as C.R. No. 430.*　　　　　　　*[G. H. Robin]*

then savour all the excitement of the ascent of Drumochter – the train locomotive in front panting stoically up the hill, the banker which had come on at Blair Athol pushing at the rear with fine determination. The sounds of steam locomotives hard at work echoed and re-echoed from the bare hillsides as the train rose higher and higher. If it was twilight or night time, the intermittent glare from open fireboxes and the showering sparks from the engine chimneys spoke of relentless exertion. Close to Dalnaspidal signalbox the banker fell back and once past the summit boards the train locomotive surged forward to run with carefree abandon down the line towards Badenoch.

The quotation from S. R. Crockett's story 'Beattock for Summit' gives a most complete and nostalgic description of banking at Beattock, or anywhere for that matter.

"The drip, drip of the rain from the carriage eaves – a silence only broken by a hissing and slow panting from the engine in front – not a noisy hissing but something quiet and apologetic as if the great blue engine did not want to break some mysterious spell. Suddenly a bump in the rear, and one looks out to find a noisy, squat impudent looking tank engine has arrived behind, blowing off steam furiously and in response from three deep hoots from the giant in front, carols joyously three or four times and starts to push the train up the hill with a gay abandon that is something to see. Up, up, through the mists until the quaintly named 'Summit Box' is reached and with a whoop from the giant in front our little travelling companion is left after labouring so noisily and well, left behind, straddling the rails, self satisfied, smug looking, but withal so self satisfied, but so utilitarian".

"Beattock for Summit" – the words remind us that they also serve who only stand and wait.

# CHAPTER SEVEN

## *Driver Jock McLeish of Perth*

D URING THE YEARS of the steam era on the railways of Britain, many enginemen became popular not only with enthusiasts but also with the travelling public. Such fame, if one may call it that, was more or less unsought by those who were concerned. The typical engineman looked on his calling merely as a job of work to be done to the best of his ability and did not consider that he was doing anything out of the ordinary.

Such a man was John McLeish of Perth, usually known as Jock, a driver from the days of the Caledonian Railway. He was well known over the Scottish system from Aberdeen to Carlisle, and in his latter years as far as Inverness on the old Highland line. Jock was of middling stature, but rather stocky in build. He had a moustache and looking every inch the textbook engine driver. He often favoured a tweed 'bunnet' which he invariably wore back to front to prevent it being blown off by the skip when he leant out from his locomotive.

I first met Jock at the time of the Second War when we fell into conversation one evening at Buchanan Street Station in Glasgow. Jock had brought in the 4.45 p.m. from Dundee, and was due to work back on the 10 p.m. to Perth. He was on the platform examining the mechanical lubricator, and he obviously relished my comment that I would not touch it – not even with a coal shovel – so hot had it become! Jock looked up recognising, I suppose, a man with inside knowledge about locomotives. When the engine came off the train we went back to the turntable outside the station and sat talking railways until it was time for him to set out for Perth again. Jock had the delightful Perth form of speech, soft-spoken and careful and, as I soon discovered, possessed an encyclopaedic knowledge of Scottish locomotive lore. As the years went past we kept in touch, with frequent visits to Perth and to my home. What days these were – the topic was 'ingins and more ingins' most of the time.

In 1902, when Jock was 13 years of age he made up his mind to leave school and go to work. Because of his liking for steam locomotives his first call was at the Caledonian Railway engine shed at Friarton in Perth, where the foreman accepted him and started him off as as 'knocker-up'. To those who do not know what this entailed it means that the knocker-up went round and wakened the men on early call. His efforts were not always well received. Let me put it in Jock's own words:

'It was just a job. I started at 8 at night until 8 in the morning, and after midnight I called round on maybe ten men – it varied from week to week. The wakener hadn't exactly a cushy job, since if he was not out on his rounds, he was a general factotum for the time office'.

This assignment lasted for roughly a year until Jock was sent to the cleaning staff, and again, let him tell my readers:

"When I went onto cleaning for good, being an old wakener I was put into what we called the 'Bogie' link. You were given a Caley passenger engine to clean – mine was No. 887 with Driver John Henderson – all the drivers had their own engines in those days".

I knew that No. 887 was a Dunalastair III, which had been St. Rollox built in 1900, and that the class had won a name for being smart pacy engines. For five years these 4–4–0s hauled the fastest Caley passenger trains over its arduous main lines. Jock continued:

"The cleaner had to come out twelve hours before the engine was to leave the shed. Some of the shifts were funny – as 887 was on the top link then, for the 5.40 a.m. to Aberdeen we came out at 5 p.m. the previous evening! Or for the 8 p.m. to Carlisle, we were out at 7.30 a.m. in the morning. I cleaned the whole engine and tender; we had to work hard, but then the Caley locomotives were turned out immaculate".

In those years, promotion was more or less by merit, as the seniority form of advancement was in the future. But it could be said with fairness that foremen and inspectors had a good eye for likely fellows among their staff. Jock had been on the cleaning staff for about three and a half years (not always on No. 887) when about 1906 he became a 'passed cleaner' available for firing duties. He was only seventeen.

"My first firing job was on old No. 493, a little Conner saddle tank which was the Perth South Yard pilot, with the harbour working thrown in. The shift started at 7 a.m. and finished about 7 p.m. The wee engine had no steam brake and the fireman had to wind the hand brake off and on when shunting. Old Bob Hall was my mate – a capricious old devil who kept his firemen working at the brake most of the time. No wonder we developed muscles!" Although the engine was only a humble 'puggie', Jock was at last on the footplate, a position which was the envy of many a teenager in those days. His sojourn on No. 493 was brief, for his sound attitude to the job had become known and he soon graduated to what were called the 'short roads'.

"I went on to the veteran 2–4–0 No. 1444 which was on the evening goods from Forfar. We took out the 7.10 p.m. passenger train, then shunted Forfar North, and made up the return train which left about 11 p.m. and got into Perth about 3 a.m. We had to shunt at most of the stations on the way in. Old Wull Hall was the driver, and one December he got off the footplate at Glamis to oil the side rods and fell into a cess pool they had been digging. It was full of water, and he was soaked to the skin. It was a bad frosty night, and before we were finished he was nearly frozen stiff, but he was a tough old sinner and said it was nought that a good dram wouldn't cure!"

Old No. 1444 had come from Dübs works in Glasgow in 1877 and found its metier in the branch line working of both passenger and goods trains until withdrawn in 1911.

It was common for the younger firemen to be sent to various outposts in the rural hinterland of Perth, such as Crieff, or Bankfoot where odd engines were stationed, and Jock had his share of these tasks too.

"I was sent to Crieff on the branch line working. Old No. 458 was the engine at the time; she was Neilson-built in 1877 and was of the 2–4–0 type. When the 0–4–4 tank No. 458 arrived on the scene in 1912, this new engine was sent to Crieff in place of the old one; the old lass was renumbered and became No. 1458, landing at Perth, where Irvine Hawkins got her for running the Liverpool goods from Perth to Dundee. Old Irvine was so fat he could hardly get in the cab door!"

Jock McLeish was gradually building up a reputation as a reliable fireman and this was noticed where it mattered. Hence his tour of the branch workings was shorter than normal and his next step up was for more serious work.

"When I came back from Crieff to Perth I found I was on the main-

[75]

line goods – in fact I was on one of the Caley 0–8–0 engines. It was No. 602 with Driver Dave Young. At first both 602 and 607 had been sent to Dundee, and then they were shifted to Perth: they brought their drivers with them. From Perth they worked to Ross Yard at Hamilton with coal traffic. This was a long day's outing, and once one of the firemen was told by the foreman that if he wanted a hair cut he'd need to change shifts with someone so he could get to a barbers before they shut! The Ross trains bound for Hamilton left Perth at 6.30 a.m. and 7.30 a.m., taking empty wagons south and they came back with loco coal for the Caley and the Highland. (Three railway companies had sheds in Perth in those days – the Caley, Highland and North British). The second train brought back a load of about twenty of the 30-ton bogie loco coal wagons. One Sunday a test train was run with these wagons, and 602 pulled 30 of them – there was an engine following a block behind in case of difficulty – but 602 sailed up Dunblane bank like no-one's business! These 0–8–0 engines were fairly heavy on coal, but one thing you can be sure of – there was no difficulty keeping steam in them, since all you had to do was to shove the coal well in behind the door!"

These were the days of ten and twelve hour shifts that did not always finish within those limits. Jock told me once that a ten hour job to Stirling and back could regularly spread over to fourteen, and yet out you came at your normal time for the next shift. Of course there were occasions when one of the Perth men stayed on the engine as long as he could to get away from the wife and her mother!

Jock was now close to his 21st birthday, and had already been recognised by the running foreman as a 'capital hand'. This was a tribute to his excellence as a conscientious workman. During 1909 Jock had moved up to the 'long road goods', as they were termed, and was usually working from Perth to Carlisle, where he booked off after a shift of some eight hours. Jock recalled that the long shifts were not helped by being shunted into almost every wayside siding to wait while three or four passenger trains went through with maybe twenty minutes between each. He once showed me a record taken in 1909 of some of the times the crews had to endure:

3 January 1909:    Fish train to Carlisle and home light: Book on Perth 3 p.m. book off Carlisle 3.45 a.m.

20 March 1909:    Sheep train to Carlisle: Book on Perth 2.15 p.m. Book off Carlisle 2.25 a.m.

21 March 1909:    (Sunday) Light engine from Carlisle. Book on Carlisle 11.25 a.m. Book off Perth 11.40 p.m.

6 August 1909:    Blairgowrie goods: Book on Perth 11.30 a.m. Book off Perth 11.50 p.m.

In later years, with the introduction of the eight hour day, locomotive-men might look askance at these hours, but before the First War, working hours in all industries were of this nature and no-one gave them a thought. As Jock was to remind me:

"You must remember that no goods went by road then: every main line goods train was out with a heavy load – often 40 to 60 wagons – and the foreman would think nothing of giving you a 'blue Jumbo' to get along with a full load to Carlisle as well as you could".

Officially there were no such engines as 'Jumbos' on the Caley, but these 0–6–0 locomotives quickly earned that nickname. A clerk in the St. Rollox drawing office once wrote about Jumbos in a report and he was curtly informed that there were six-coupled engines painted blue and Westinghouse fitted, and there were six-coupled engines painted black with the steam brake, and as to Jumbos, there were none!

As time marched on Jock McLeish moved from the Caley 0–6–0s on to the passenger links, and his principal recollection of this period was sharing duties on the Caledonian superheated 4–4–0 No. 133 with Driver Peter Thompson or 'Big Pete', as he was called. This locomotive belonged to the 139 class, often referred to as the Dunalastair IVs of 1911.

"When we got the superheaters, (ours was the third that came to Perth) we were told they'd make a big difference going to Carlisle. We left with the 8 p.m. sleepers from the north, and came back with the down 'Tourist'. It was a hefty night's work and for the 300 miles from Perth to Carlisle and back there were no mileage payments for us. At the end of a six night-week, my wages were only 37/6d. But 133 was a great engine. The trick with a superheater was to get the brick arch hot before leaving, and not to start cold. Even with that, leaving Carlisle, a saturated engine would make better time to Beattock than a superheater, but we would always have the edge on the bank itself".

Jock told me about a Sunday morning when Big Pete and he were working on the 'Tourist' with No. 133. Going down Auchterarder bank, they were passing the mile posts after Whitemoss at from 11 to 12 second intervals and doing this while hauling a train of some 300 tons on Jock's reckoning. As he observed, 'This was gey fast', and in fact at 75–85 mph it was the fastest he had ever travelled up to that time. In his experience these superheaters were all very free running engines especially downhill.

"And the superheaters fairly saved coal and water. We could do Perth to Carlisle and back on about 4½ tons of coal. A tank of water would take her both ways. Mind we were non-stop to Stirling, and if the Oban portion ran separately we did Perth non-stop. Big Pete would not let you run with the boiler filled up: 'Hauf a gless', he used to say, 'An' gie me dry steam, that's what shoves her along'."

Jock admired the superheaters and thought the Caley 139 class were beauties. There were simple rules of operating based on experience that became part of the daily round:

"When we left Perth going south, Big Pete would say, 'Noo lad, nae injectors on till we pass Whitemoss box an' full her up for toppin' the bank at Blackford' – and we never lost steam, for 133 would steam against the injector anytime".

When the First War came, after the initial 'business as usual' phase, the railways were overwhelmed with a rush of traffic which nearly brought them to a standstill. Jock recounted many experiences of his war years on the Caley but one will suffice by way of illustration.

"It was during 1915, when I was still on the shovel side that I was booked out with Jock Drury to take a special to Carlisle. We had No. 46, another superheated 4–4–0, and we left Perth at 2.45 a.m. on a Sunday with no less than 34 vans. We got to Carlisle about 12 of the day, and booked off at Kingmoor and went to the dormitory until called. At 7 p.m. word came to take a troop train coming off the Lanky (Lancashire & Yorkshire) at about 9 p.m. to Perth. We booked on and made 46 ready: then we sat in the Citadel station until 11.30 p.m. when the troop train at last came in. We left at 12.30 a.m., and got to Perth at 5.50 a.m., only to be told we'd get a conductor and we'd have to take it up the Heilan' as far as Aviemore! They had only one engine left in the Heilan' shed and it was under repair. The Heilan' was desperate for engines in the First War Years. So we got a Drummond Jumbo in place of 46, and we set sail. It was a sair fecht for a Jumbo to take a troop train up Drumochter, and we got to Aviemore at 4 in the afternoon. Jock Drury says to me, 'We'll just leave the engine and take anything home', and so we did. We got on a goods going south, and the pair of us slept in the brake van. We had to be wakened at Perth! No wonder – from Carlisle to Aviemore we had been on the footplate for over twenty-one hours!" They had covered over 240 miles, 90 of them with a hard-pressed Jumbo.

Wartime experiences of a similar nature were common among enginemen in those years and after all, as Jock put it, "Nae man bothered much aboot it". Towards the end of the First War, the railway unions saw that with promises being so lavishly made by politicians about 'a land fit for heroes', there was now an opportunity for making railway service less of a trial and accordingly the eight hour day became the main claim. Wages had increased during the war years by what was known as the war bonus, but after 1918 there were attempts to reduce it or remove it altogether. This short-sighted action on the part of the railway companies caused considerable trouble with staff, which culminated in the strike of September 1919.

Jock McLeish had by this time become what was termed a 'passed fireman', but such a rank meant that 320 driving turns had yet to be amassed before he could be appointed a driver. The 1919 agreement on the eight hour day did mean, however, that men like Jock McLeish found promotion came fairly rapidly as staff in all grades was increased by a third. It was not long, therefore, before Jock became a passed driver:

"My first engine in 1919 was No. 591, a blue Caley Jumbo dating from 1897. We had three or four jobs on our hands: We worked the 6.35 a.m. from Perth to Coupar Angus, shunting all the sidings out and back, lifting traffic for Perth as required. Twice or three times a week we worked the Pitnappie branch – that's what we called the Dundee to Alyth line, as there was a siding called Pitnappie on it and that gave it its name".

"Then there was the morning goods to Lochearnhead, the evening goods to Coupar, and sometimes a conditional run to Stirling. Canny jobs every one of them".

"After a year or so, I got a new engine – No. 319, one of the Pickersgill 0-6-0 goods engines of 1919. People called them 'tin cans' but that was rubbish. They were sound engines, although the piston valves spoiled them when they were saturated, as they could not pull like a slide valve engine, but when they were superheated they were all right. We had the road van goods to Forfar and back, and on Friday nights we went to Aberdeen where we booked off, and then came back on the Saturday night. We had two workings to Stirling mostly to bring back coal, and we also had a working to Dundee. "In those days there were eight sidings between Perth and Dundee serving the needs of the farming communities, of coal merchants, potato merchants, brickworks, or summer activities such as berry picking.

Jock recollected this run from his earlier years. "When I was a young fireman about 1907, I was on this same route with an old lad called 'Bugler' Dunn or 'The Tank' (he'd a belly blawn up wi' beer). We had an old 0-4-2 engine on it, No. 1332 – an old stager of Neilsons from the early seventies – and we used to leave Perth about 7.30 a.m. and often did not finish until 7.30 p.m. Fancy spending all that time going to Dundee and back! Of course there was a lot of time idling at wayside stations, and old Bugler used to take his fishing rod wi' him and try a cast or two on the burn at Inchture. These were the days – nae control to bother you! But there were big changes coming in the twenties".

In 1923 the railway amalgamations took place, and as Jock pointed out there was an upheaval around the end of 1924 when nearly all the links were recast. The Caley's big superheated 4-6-0s, Nos. 184 and 187, were put on the Perth-Carlisle goods roster; they were joined by two of the River class Nos. 942 and 943 which were also placed on that route:

"The Perth-Carlisle goods were three single-home turns worked by two Perth engines night about. 942 and 943 were grand engines – when they came out new in 1916 they were put on passenger work and they were the best thing in locomotives for passenger working that ever ran out of Perth, but when Pickersgill's 64 and 65 came along in 1917, the River class were taken off and they never ran a passenger train again until during the Second War. 942 became one of my engines when I was on the Carlisle link. Then the new LMS 60 class was built – they were modelled on the Pickersgill 4-6-0s – and I transferred to one of them. Soon the 'common user' set-up started and you had to take any-thing on wheels that was thought fit for the job".

At times there were some controversial issues at Perth shed, as Jock explained:

"When the through Crewe to Perth run began, some of the Perth men wanted to work to Crewe alternate with the Crewe men so the boss sent me to Carlisle with an engine pass to Crewe to see how long it would take to learn the road. From Carlisle to Preston was fairly easy but Preston to Crewe was tricky. I said when I got back that three weeks would do – a week for Preston and two more weeks for Crewe. Or else I thought a week to go over the road and four to five weeks with a conductor. But it never came to anything".

Jock was on the Perth-Carlisle goods link for a number of years, interrupted by a move on to what was called the 'spare link' where, due to his extraordinary knowledge of routes, he came in useful for all kinds of workings.

Surprisingly Jock McLeish had very little to say about the Second War years; he was mainly on passenger and troop train rosters, but he had many comments about engine classes, of which the following is a sample:

"Black Fives were one of the finest lot of engines ever built. They could handle anything. Jubilees? Well, I didn't like them as they were bad steamers and the inside cylinder was only good for giving the pre-paration crew more work. As to Pacifics, the Duchess ones were the best Pacifics ever built; the Lizzies were good enough but the Duchesses beat the lot. We used to get them at times on the Aberdeen run when they came off the Night Postal, and they could tackle anything that was

A 956 Class locomotive takes shape in the erecting shop at St. Rollox in the
summer of 1921.                                                    [A. E. Glen]

My boss, the fitter Bill Crooks, at the steam shed at St. Rollox working on
No. 956, the first of the Caley's big 4–6–0 superheaters in 1921. The engine
was in works grey prior to testing.                               [A. E. Glen]

Polmont shed was a timber structure with five roads for locomotives. In L.N.E.R. years it was the base for former North British engines such as J 36 or J 37 0–6–0 which were used on coal or freight haulage in the area.

[A. G. Ellis Collection]

N2 tank B.R. No. 69507 makes heavy weather of the incline as it passes Parkhead on a Hyndland – Shettleston train in June 1958.  [G. H. Robin]

aung on ahint them".

Jock of course knew some techniques of engine craft that were
unique. Once when I was visiting him in Perth I happened to mention
that I had never travelled on the footplate from the Fair City to Aberdeen. "Bide over till Monday and come wi' me", was Jock's answer.
"I'm on the down T.P.O." This was the travelling post office or 'the
Postal' as it was called, leaving Perth at 6.27 a.m. and travelling non-
stop to Aberdeen, arriving there at 8 a.m. We had a Black Five that
Monday, and approaching Guthrie Jock suddenly shut off steam except
for a cushion breath and the engine began to slow down gradually. I
was standing beside the fireman and asked him what was going on, and
he told me to go over behind Jock and watch. I did so and saw we were
approaching a 'C' board with a '20' above it; we were doing just about
that. When we had fully passed the 'T' board, and Jock had checked
that the tail of the train was clear of the slack he opened the regulator
again and off we blasted north. Afterwards when I asked him about
this, Jock replied, "Ony idiot could brake for a slow but let the engine
dae it hersel – she'll make a better job o' it". This was just one of his
knowledgeable touches that made him the expert engineman he was.

On our trip with the Postal from Perth I asked Jock about keeping
time. "Man, I have timing points", he said: these were Stanley Junction,
Eassie, Forfar, Guthrie Junction, Kinnaber, and Carmont – this latter
giving him his approximate time of arrival in Aberdeen. Let Jock re-
count his timing points from Glasgow: "If I'm going oot o' Buchanan
Street for Perth my first point is Lenzie Mill Box near Cumbernauld. I
ken then that at my next which is Larbert Junction that I'll be a minute
or so in hand at Larbert station if we have to stop. After Stirling I hae
twa – Blackford and Whitemoss box – and I ken then if I'll be in Perth
on time".

As the years went on, Jock McLeish worked mostly on passenger
train rosters, visiting Aberdeen, Carlisle, Edinburgh, Carstairs or Glasgow, and even latterly Inverness, for the Perth sheds had become one.
Then in the summer of 1951, the B.R. Standard 'Fives' Nos. 73005 to
73009 came to Perth, and were at once put into the top links with each
locomotive being double manned. The workings were arranged thus:
Perth to Glasgow and return, then remanned; Perth to Aberdeen and
return. This pattern was followed for each engine, and the standard of
working was a vast improvement on the 'common user' system. Jock
liked the 'Standards' very much. Retirement from the railway loomed
on the horizon, however, and one day in 1954 he had his last working
on the footplate to Aberdeen; on the return to Perth his engine was
remanned to go on to Glasgow, and 'Auld Jock' thus completed a

*A B.R. Standard Class 5 (No. 73006) storms past Balornock shed as it makes for Stirling. These locomotives were worked on a two-team basis at Perth and were popular with all the engine crews.* [A. G. Ellis]

career which had given him a life full of satisfaction.

I once asked him what in his opinion was the best engine he was ever on. Jock thought for a few moments, then came the answer I had half expected, "I wid say Caley 133 wi' big Pete; these were the best all-rounders we ever had". His days as a fireman on that superb Caledonian locomotive had made a lasting impression on Jock:

"Firing the 'Tourist' wi' 133 was not too bad at all. Mind the tank in the big bogie tender held 4,600 gallons and we always filled the boiler and topped the tank at the Citadel station in Carlisle. Man, we were often through Kirtlebridge before the injector went on. But for firing, the superheaters were a bit of cake, if you knew how to humour them! I used to watch the back corners, for if you got a hole there you were bang in trouble".

These were only a few of Jock's shrewd comments after 48 years on the footplate, 35 of them as an engine driver, and how far removed from text books and formulae his long and varied experience was. After his retirement I used to visit him and nothing delighted me more than to sit in his garden with some of his cronies and listen to the most fascinating talk about 'ingins' that one could wish to hear. Jock was blessed with a remarkable memory and to spend any time in his company was enjoyable for the shrewd and knowledgeable comments he made about his railway recollections of men and locomotives.

# CHAPTER EIGHT

## A Fitter's Choice

MOST MEN WHO are able to fulfil a youthful ambition in their choice of work are blessed with contentment. I wanted to work with steam locomotives, and no doubt would have been unhappy anywhere else. I was to find much satisfaction in my work, but an engine shed was not a pleasure ground. They were built to house locomotives, a utilitarian purpose with little or no concern for the welfare of those who were to work in them. At least the drivers and firemen spent little of their time in the sheds, but the servicing staffs who provided the essential services for the running crews had to spend almost their entire shifts in the places. We often worked in deplorable conditions – cramped, filthy and ill-lit. We all grumbled but nevertheless had to get on with the job.

The problems of locomotive maintenance at a running shed were greatly accentuated by the lack of proper tools and materials to do the job. On my first visit to London I went to the Science Museum at South Kensington to view "Puffing Billy" and "Rocket". I walked round and stood in admiration at the thought of the engineers who had built those locomotives without machine tools or modern materials, but believe me often in my places of work I was in much the same situation as these locomotive pioneers.

Let me review some of the other sheds where I went to work. First comes Polmont, to which I went in the 1930's. It had been opened by the North British Railway in 1915. Polmont's workings once embraced Dundee and Carlisle via the Border counties line through Riccarton Junction and Berwick to Hexham. The latter route was assigned to the former N.B.R. Class S (L.N.E.R. Class J37), which were Reid's super-heated 0-6-0s. The principal workings in my time, however, were to Cadder (near Lenzie) and South Leith.

Polmont was closed in the early 1960s. During its final years, the number of steam engines in traffic was much reduced. These consisted of two L.N.E.R. J38 0-6-0s for hauling coal trains from Kinneil to Ravenscraig, plus about six former N.B.R. class S engines (J37) for general workings in the local area. By the 1950s all the shunting engines (or pilots as we preferred to call them) – some ex-N.B.R. 0-6-2 tanks and several old N.B.R. Class G 0-4-0 saddle tanks (L.N.E.R. Class Y) – had been replaced by B.R. Class 06 or 08 shunters. The latter were known locally as 'bulldogs'.

Latterly, Polmont shed served as a storage depot for withdrawn engines mostly awaiting scrapping. These consisted of Director class 4-4-0s, some B1s, plus a motley collection of L.M.S.R. 2-6-2 tanks, in company with former C.R. Drummond Jumbos.

Another shed which I came to know well was Yoker, in Glasgow's dockland. This old Caledonian shed had been opened about the same time as Rothesay Dock on the north bank of the Clyde. Its activity was very much geared to the needs of the port, but at times its engines worked cattle trains to Gorgie market in Edinburgh as well as iron ore trains to Gartsherrie near Coatbridge.

My final assignment was at Parkhead shed which was built by the Edinburgh & Glasgow Railway in the early 1860s. Long ago, its locomotives worked to Dundee and Grangemouth, and had the major share of the North British Railway coal traffic in Lanarkshire. Parkhead also took the brunt of the N.B.R. substantial suburban services in the Glasgow area. In its final years, the shed had very few steam engines apart from those on the scrap line. Several 0-6-2 tanks were still in service, and a few of the durable J36 class 0-6-0s, which were eventually sent to Bathgate, were also there.

These J36 engines were among my favourites. They were typical 'general utility' locomotives which both the L.N.E.R. and L.M.S.R. inherited in abundance. The 18 inch 0-6-0s designed by Holmes for the N.B.R. and subsequently rebuilt by Reid, and the larger Drummond Jumbos of the Caledonian Railway endured well into the 1960s. All were simple, straight-forward engines, solidly built and free from annoying gadgets. They became maids-of-all-work on both lines. For all-round performance and reliability, they outclassed any other locomotives in service. Their generous boiler power, high adhesion and relatively small driving wheels were well suited to lines with steep inclines, where the 0–6–0s were equally capable of pulling passenger or freight trains.

These classes were not usually described as flyers, but amazing speed records were always a basis for tall stories among enginemen. In pre-1914 years Dawsholm shed in north-west Glasgow, which housed several 0–6–0s, was accustomed to send one daily to Brocketsbrae in Lanarkshire to uplift a train of milk churns. There was a substantial milk traffic into Glasgow by rail from the country districts around the city at that time. It was the regular assignment of Driver Burrell and one morning after picking up the vehicles he arrived at Lesmahagow Junction signalbox, where it was customary to hold the milk train to allow a down London express to pass. On this particular morning, however, the express was twenty minutes late, and so the signalman agreed to allow the milk train to go through providing it could keep well out of the way. Now Driver Burrell had a Drummond 0–6–0, Westinghouse-fitted – a 'blue Jumbo' if you prefer – and on getting the road he set off at the double. According to the train crew's story they went through Uddingston, Newton and Cambuslang at over 80 mph! This, of course, was quite an achievement with an engine on 5ft. wheels. The churns got such a jolly good rattling that on arrival in Glasgow the crew reported that they were carrying a cargo of butter!

On the L.N.E.R., J36 was the class number given to the old N.B.R. Class C, and the group comprised 168 locomotives. The L.M.S.R. had 242 of the former Caley Jumbos (230 in the original C.R. territory plus 12 on the Highland section): both varieties were long lasting.

I first came to know the Holmes engines at Polmont, and they possessed some features which are worth placing on record. The design, both in the original and rebuilt forms, was very simple; there were no attempts at clever engineering, for apart from the N.B.R. Atlantics, Cowlairs did not go in for that! For the type of workings on which they were used ease of maintenance was all important. You have to remember that much of their time was spent on 'pilot' working. Now in Scotland, as I have remarked, this need not involve the piloting of trains, but is the prosaic task of shunting in yards. Sometimes the J36s were 'running pilots' – that is, they combined shunting with short trips between yards, usually to visit collieries or other works.

Many of these locomotives would leave their home depot on a Sunday around midnight and would not return until the week was over, unless they made a trip midweek for coal or other stores. As they were frequently employed for three shifts, it will be realised that a power of work was accomplished in the course of 24 hours.

Mechanically these Scottish 0–6–0s were of sound construction: everything of importance for routine maintenance was easily accessible. The only time the J36s gave excessive trouble was during the Second World War when for some absurd notion, the closed slide bars were replaced by open bars; at the same time the soft-packed piston and spindle glands were fitted with twin cast-iron packing rings. These were major mistakes. The type of white metalling on the crosshead broke off easily, causing 'lift' in the crosshead itself, while the open bars made matters worse. The glands blew almost continuously. These were fed from capillary siphons and when the two small oil cups were empty that was that. The drivers were fed up by the state of affairs, and just let the glands blow.

If properly lubricated by force-feed, cast-iron packing rings were quite successful but on engines which had only two small oil cups supplying the piston rods, the system could never work. Much time and energy was wasted for a couple of years until there was a reversion to soft packing. The performance must have run up a huge bill in time and materials as well as taking locomotives off the road when they were most required.

The boilers on these 0–6–0s were of robust construction and gave ease in steam raising. The only exceptions were the locomotives which were fitted with spark arresters to comply with regulations governing their working through areas of Forestry Commission plantations. These spark arresters were of different types but one of the favourites was a cone-shaped wire basket which fitted on top of the blast pipe and continued into the petticoat above it, thus effectively destroying the blast of the fire. Complaints to the powers that be were useless; after all, regulations were there to be obeyed. The drivers and fitters, however, were wont to take the law into their own hands and throw the contraption out, taking a chance that nothing untoward would happen in woodland areas. If the missing spark arresters came to notice there were carpetings galore, but on reflection the people responsible for the crazy apparatus should have been on the carpet in the first place for making the locomotives unworkable.

For passenger rosters on branch lines the J36s, which were fitted with continuous brakes, were ideal. They could cope with trains of moderately heavy stock numbering some six or seven coaches with confidence. At times they were pressed into service on heavier assignments as substitutes for failed locomotives of greater power. I remember an example of this which occurred during the Glasgow Fair in 1938. Parkhead shed had allocated a Reid superheater J37 0–6–0 to work a special from Bridgeton Cross Station to Crail in Fife. Half an hour before the time for leaving the shed, some trouble arose with the vacuum ejector on this engine and J36 No. 9772, which was likewise dual-fitted, was substituted. This engine had been built at Cowlairs in 1900. So it came about that driver Colin Gray and fireman Robert Duncan set out with what they considered to be a most unsuitable engine to work a train of nine non-corridor coaches. All these were well filled with excursionists. The first stop was scheduled for Dalmeny. Colin Gray was one of these enginemen who delighted in a challenge, and this assignment was certainly that. Much to the team's amazement not only did No. 9772 keep time but actually improved upon it, although as Robert Duncan said, "The b . . . . . tender was b . . . . . well stripped by the time we got to Crail!"

Prior to the numerous branch line closures in the Glasgow area, these J36s could be found on passenger services to Aberfoyle, Helensburgh or Balloch. Some were seen on the Forth and Clyde section from Stirling to Balloch. For this type of working many engines were fitted with tender cabs, while others had weather boards for running tender first.

Representatives of the J36 class could be seen at almost every former North British shed. Some of them had gone to these places when new, returned to them when rebuilt, and then completed their service there. During the First World War, twenty five were sent to France for use by the Railway Operating Division , and on their return were named after people and places connected with the campaign. One of the names selected was that of the famed cartoon character, *Ole Bill*. Afterwards there was hardly anyone named Bill in the locomotive department of the old N.B. who did not claim that the engine had been named after him!

Both the Caledonian and the North British Railways made further developments of their basic 0–6–0 classes. The McIntosh Standard Goods of the 18½ inch type had larger boilers and totalled 96 while Pickersgill had a further 55 constructed; latterly these were superheated. The N.B.R. also built engines with 18½ inch cylinders to a Reid design, all of which were subsequently superheated. The Reid J37 class consisted of 104 locomotives, big-boilered superheaters, which represented the largest development of the basic Drummond design. All these engines did excellent work until steam began to disappear. The J37s were greatly favoured by the men who took both passenger and goods trains over the West Highland line, where their gradient-climbing abilities were put to regular gruelling tests which they easily met.

On the Caledonian section, the McIntosh engines were working main line goods trains right up to the Second World War. It is on record that one of these went as new in 1901 to a shed, and twenty two years afterwards it was still there on the same working in the charge of the same driver! In contrast to the McIntosh Standard Goods which were successes from the start, the Pickersgill variety which were saturated had a dubious reputation, as Jock McLeish knew well, until they were superheated. A vast improvement in their performance then took place.

All of the 0–6–0s were commonly described by the enginemen as 'Jumbos', a term which perfectly summed up the elephantine type of work which they performed. Two examples of the Scottish 0–6–0s have been preserved: N.B.R. No. 673 *Maude*, a First War R.O.D. veteran, is in the care of the Scottish Railway Preservation Society, while C.R. No. 828, a Standard Goods which is owned by the Scottish Locomotive Preservation Trust Fund, is now at Aviemore.

Plenty of other locomotive types came into my care. Many of these were 'foreigners' from south of the Border, and some of them stand out in my recollection. Much has been written in praise of the Gresley engines of the L.N.E.R. Most of these caught the eye; many of them performed outstandingly, but what did we fitters think of them?

Let us begin with the K2 class of 2–6–0s. Most of my readers will be unaware that if the vacuum chamber rolling rings had to be renewed (and that was quite often), the engine and tender had first to be separated; this was essential in order to dismantle the chambers before these could be opened up to expose the rings themselves. The piston also had to be removed. Think of the thousands of man-hours of effort involved all over the L.N.E.R. system in this time-wasting performance. If some thought had been given to reversing the position of the chamber covers, the piston could have been removed from the bottom.

The K2s also had trailing sand boxes located behind the trailing wheel below the cab, with the filling hole on the cab floor of all places. After the fireman had sloshed water all over the floor, the drivers would complain that the sands would not work. No wonder, for they were soaking wet! If the trailing sand box had been placed (as was the leading box) between the frames clear of the cab, the sands at least would have been dry.

Another troublesome feature of the K2 was the exhaust steam injector. This was mounted in a really inaccessible position below the footplate, and had to be taken to bits every time anything went wrong with it. Is it surprising that the fitters appreciated the wit of the chap who referred to these engines as 'Ragtimers'?

Among the locomotives which were the despair of Scottish fitters, ame the Gresley-designed 0–6–2 tanks of the N2 class, which were familiarly known as 'teddy bears' – why I do not know. The majority of these were employed on the London suburban services from Kings Cross, and were highly spoken of there. The few that were sent up to the Glasgow area were not liked by anyone. Performance wise and in other ways they were failures.

The first snag was steaming trouble, which could be ascribed to the Gresley twinheader superheater, a continual source of bother. In spite of all the attention we gave the device, it was never satisfactory in my opinion.

The Gresley superheater was a trouble maker because the elements were jointed to the headers by means of a stud that held the element joint in position within a circular groove in the header. This had a copper washer. The action of the blast, plus the fact that the smoke box ash acted like a grinding powder, soon had the metal round the groove pitted and worn. It then became virtually impossible to keep the element joints tight. To make matters worse, the top header was fixed to the boiler while the bottom one was fixed to the frames. As a result the front end slackened in service because the top and bottom pulled against each other and this caused the element joint to blow – a constant complaint in the drivers' journals. This fault was bound to make the locomotives steam badly and on many occasions it could bring them to a standstill with the boiler pressure in double figures! After the maintenance of the 'teddy bears' became the responsibility of Inverurie works, boilers supplied by Doncaster were fitted with Robinson superheaters and the Gresley originals went to the scrap heap.

Another infuriating feature of the N2s was the gudgeon pin that coupled the small end of the connecting rod to the crosshead. It was put in position from *inside* the slide bars, the nut for the screwed end of the pin being between the frames and the slide bars. This nut was tightened up by inserting a box key through a hole in the frame. So far so good, but the nut had the bad habit of striking the leading horn block, which either broke off or was badly damaged. The number of times we had to clean up the damaged threads with a file (we had no other method or means of doing this) was legion. After 1948, at least on Scottish Region, the engineers saw fit to arrange for the pin to be put in the opposite way. Maintenance became much easier, for the nut breaking ceased, but it took twenty five years to think out that solution.

The large ends of the connecting rods on the N2 were of the strap type with a tapered cotter to bring the brasses together and two tapered bolts to hold the strap. The taper was said to be in the region of 1 in 108, and the bolts had the habit of seizing up. When that happened we had to bore them out, very often using nothing better than a hand ratchet and drill. Bolts of a uniform size made to a 'tapping' fit would have held just as well and prevented a lot of wasted effort.

The N2 piston glands were kept in position by no less than *six* $7/8$ inch studs with double nuts and split pins for good measure. To us these refinements were quite superfluous; we contrasted them with our own engines where piston glands were normally fixed by two $1/8$th inch studs with double nuts and no split pins, and they never came adrift.

For their part the drivers disliked the N2s. They waltzed uncertainly along the track, and after an engine overturned on the Hamilton line, a speed limit of 45 mph was clamped on them. There were also a number of restrictions on where they could run, which limited their operational usefulness. Whilst the London engine crews may have been happy with the 0–6–2 tanks, up in Scotland they were 'a soo wi' anither snoot', and were treated as such.

Latterly the 'teddy bears' appeared on local goods workings where any failures would not snarl up the system. By this time, the far larger and more efficient Gresley three-cylinder 2–6–2 tanks were arriving to take over local workings, thus bringing sighs of relief to the enginemen and fitters. Around 1957 or so some of the remaining 'teddy bears' were ordered to be sent to the former LMS shed at Dawsholm, but their notoriety had gone before them. I remember an irate shed foreman phoning me to ask if we thought that his place was the local scrap yard. I really could not blame him, although some of his own locomotives were scarcely in the pink of condition. One of the N2s was used at Eastfield for carriage warming at Cowlairs siding while at Parkhead Shed another was kept as a stationary boiler for washing-out when the regular shed boiler was having repairs. It is quite likely that the motive power people thought that in both instances these N2s were best out of the way.

The three-cylinder 2–6–2 tanks of the V1 and V3 classes were not without their vices. The trailing sand boxes were in the cab but against the back plate this time – so no wet sand problems. The pipe went down through the cab floor to the rear of the trailing wheel. So far so good: the pipe was fixed to studs on the bottom of the box which, after lifting the floor boards, was quite accessible. The pipe, however, was in halves, with a joint in the middle. To take the pipe out for renewal or to make a repair half way down meant splitting the joint. This entailed a major engineering exercise – first taking off the cab foot steps and then dismantling the equalizing pipe that ran behind the steps from the front tank to the rear! All this to undo two $1/2$" bolts that held the halves of the pipe together. What fun we had! The leading sanders on these ngines had a sleeve valve inside the box which was an unmitigated nuisance as the holes in the sleeve easily choked, and the poor fitter had to balance on a frame cross stretcher to clear the sleeves by means of a wire.

Other examples of design nonsense were the Gresley pull-out regulator handles and fitments. These were advantageous from one point of view – the driver's – but when you visit a Gresley locomotive, have a close look at the cab fitments. Ask yourself how are the joints on either side of the box in the middle to be renewed? It will perhaps cause astonishment when you learn that various pipes had to be removed, plus one of the carrying brackets for the cross rod before the joints could be split. If one of them had blown out, *both* had to be renewed, since the studs that held them in place were moveable – they had to be to get them into position at all!

These design weaknesses made work for us, but this was nothing to our labours with our old friends, the vacuum rolling rings on the V1 and V3 tanks. In this case, the cab floor boards had to be taken up. The injector feed and delivery pipes had then to be removed as these crossed the cab floor. After that we had to lift the cab floor itself, uncouple all the brake rigging below it, and hoist up the brake cylinders by means of a block and tackle dropped through a hole in the cab roof. What a carry on this was – a full 8 hours of work at the best of times.

Before enthusiasts rush to justify such design arrangements, or to complain of poor maintenance, think of the inadequacies of the locomotive designs with which fitters had to cope. All three classes of Gresley tanks (N2, V1 and V3) were fitted with open slide bars which also gave plenty of trouble. Ask any fitter who had to renew the front holding bolts on an N2 slide bars how he liked that job, and believe me, the epithets will surely start to flow.

The J38 and J39 0–6–0s were not exactly fault free, either. Firstly they had the same gudgeon pins as the N2; after giving years of trouble these were altered in the same way. The main shortcomings in the J38/39 engines were the insufficient bearing surfaces and, within three months of being 'shopped', the J38s in particular were classic examples of the 'shake, rattle and roll' variety.

On Gresley engines there was a device known as the reversing tension spring, which was mounted on the reversing shaft to counterbalance the gear. This was a spiral spring set in a groove on the shaft; an adjusting bolt was fixed to two lugs on the end of the spring through a hole in the cross stretcher. When the spring broke, the whole shaft had to be uncoupled and taken down. Whilst five minutes took off the old spring and put on the new, it took at least *five hours* to do the rest.

When Thompson became Chief Mechanical Engineer, he fixed the adjusting screw to lugs on the shaft on his locomotives; he put the screw through the cross stretcher and fixed an ordinary spiral spring on th stretcher. The result was that if a spring broke about ten minute sufficed to complete its renewal.

Surprisingly, a N2/2 has been preserved at the Great Central Railway at Loughborough, but VIs and V3s are absent from the list. I am sure that enthusiasts will have plenty to keep them entertained on the N2 a that example is also condenser-fitted.

There was clearly a lack of communication between the design team and the shed fitters. We were never consulted, and it frequently took years for our observations to filter through to the higher echelons. shall not touch upon such sore points as centre large ends, conjugated gears, relief cocks on Gresley Pacifics or other items. Did designers eve ask themselves, "How are our fitters to service and maintain the locomotives?" Very rarely, might be the answer.

When the B.R. Standard classes were at the planning stage, the Railway Executive had a mock-up of the cab built and brought drivers from all quarters to look at it. These men were asked to give their opinion on such matters as the position of the steam brake handle. Was it placed so that they could reach it without having to shift their fat rear ends off the comfy seats? This was very participative, but you should have heard the derisive laughter from the maintenance staffs. While the brake handle might have been 'just right', the pipes leading away from it had jointing nuts in such an awkward position between the boiler and the cab that poor fitters were tied in knots trying to reach them whenever the nuts required rejointing! I know because I was one of them. Yes, we got on with the job, meanwhile criticising the designers for all we were worth, but they never asked us what *we* thought about their engines. Had they asked me, my advice would have been, 'Make it easy to maintain'.

# CHAPTER NINE

## *The Running Shed*

WHEN I WAS a chargehand fitter at Parkhead in the early 1950s, every shift was sure to present me with a set of new problems. To take an example, I remember a typical afternoon shift. The problems began before I had even reached the shed for on my way up the lane at about 1.45 p.m. I met a driver who complained that the steam brake on his engine was giving trouble. Well, I made a mental note to look into the matter.

In our small office which adjoined the running foreman's room I found my colleague who had been on duty since 6 a.m. According to him it had been a quiet morning: "It's all in the log, so it's over to you bud, and the best of British!" So saying he rose to leave.

The log book was an institution. It contained full notes on the work done during a shift, with red ink comments jotted in by the shedmaster at his daily examination of its contents just for good measure! I always looked through it, registering the main points, and on this occasion I noted that the shed master wanted to see me.

After that I checked with the timekeeper to see that all my shift were present – three fitters plus their mates, and my examiner who acted as my deputy. There was also a 'periodical' fitter with his mate and a fourth year apprentice to make up the team. The former carried out the work involved at the 20,000 mile periodical examinations, consisting mainly of piston valve and motion inspections. Another fitter was also available but only up to 4.30 p.m.: this was the 'ile man', whose forte was attention to mechanical and hydrostatic lubricators, axle box oil keeps and such like fittings, which kept him fully employed.

I was on my way to speak to the running foreman when the timekeeper hurried in with a 'phone message which read "Charlie Stewart wants a fitter at the Junction Box at 2.35 p.m.: right injector not working". Although I often felt like consigning the Stewart clan to outer darkness, I sent a cleaner to fetch Jimmy, who was one of my best fitters and his mate. They would go over to the box to rescue Stewart's engine.

On the subject of injectors, there were many local expressions for parts of a locomotive. In the Glasgow area 'jerry' was the common term for an injector. Laconic comments that "The jerries isna workin'" were a cue for me to get busy.

When I was at Parkhead I remember a locomotive in the yard which was exciting an unusual amount of attention. The train crew seemed unduly agitated. First, they summoned a fitter to join them. Before long a foreman was also on the footplate. From the engine on which I was working, I watched all this activity with growing interest. What was up? Shortly there was a shout, "See here Alan – the jerries isna' workin'!" I went across, took a look at the gauges, and the 'jerries' were certainly not working, but no wonder. I picked up the coal shovel and gave the tender tank a hearty swipe – it rang like a bell – it was empty! There were a few red faces on that footplate, but the cure was simple – just fill up the tank . . .

At Parkhead shed, above an office door there was a framed notice, "Yours the credit; ours the blame", which neatly summed up our situation. Our praises were rarely sung. A useful rule in running shed work was never to cross a bridge until it was right in front. What bridges had we to cross that day? Well, the repair cards showed few major problems on hand, but the examiner might just find a broken spring or something worse. Seven passenger trains had to go out between 2.30 p.m. and 4.40 p.m., plus six goods engines up to 6 p.m. Now that Jimmy was over at the junction, the other men would continue with work in progress – finishing repairs to locomotives washed out during the forenoon or fitting a new vacuum train pipe on a defective engine.

Just after 2.30 p.m., when I looked out from my office window, I saw Jimmy clambering onto Stewart's engine and hoped that it would be a straightforward job, with no call for a fresh locomotive. Anyway, such thoughts vanished when the timekeeper banged a mug of strong lack tea on my desk. There was a good team at Parkhead – we had been together for some years, and our fitters went round the shifts the opposite way from us and so we saw the whole staff in rotation.

After sipping my tea, I went along to see the Shed master; the chief clerk showed me into his room. Some opening remarks brought us to the heart of the matter. A Gresley derived gear was causing excessive overtravel on the centre piston valve. What could I suggest? I explained that as all holes for the pins were bushed, it would mean sending to Darlington for a complete set of bushes, and once the worn lot were removed, the replacements could be pressed into place. As I was about to leave, I was told about an enquiry relating to the number of engines we had which were fitted with Klinger gauge cocks. I had to refer to my notebook – the answer was '14 passenger engines, 4 goods engines, plus 2 pugs', which happened to be former N.B.R. 0–6–2 tanks.

Back in my office again, I found that the examiner had collected new repair cards and put them in the slotted box which carried the fitters' names. Cards for work which had been completed were signed and dumped in a box on the desk. When a driver came off duty, he wrote up any repairs on a card which was put into the time office for the foreman to collect.

The afternoon wore on and Jimmy returned with Driver Stewart's engine; according to the former, some train crews were "bloomin' idiots". At least they could have shut the tank valve and cleared the strainer in the feed water pipe for a start! Nevertheless, I left word in the log book for the night staff to clean out the engine's tank. I also wrote a note for the shed master to find out from the drivers on the engine (it was double shifted) where they were taking water as there must be an exceptionally dirty tank somewhere along the line.

Meanwhile the previous night's washouts were being blown down outside. A fitter came to tell me that the brake cylinder bolts on old No. 9210, one of our 0–6–2 tanks, would require renewal, and that he had told the outside foreman to leave it 'off the board' for a time – in other words, to take it out of service. This engine had been built by the North British Locomotive Company in 1910, and it ran until 1958.

I had been waiting for Jimmy to tell him that our Black Five, No. 44791, had a defective injector feed bag and a broken driving spring. As she was to go on the 8 p.m. fast goods to Newcastle, activity would be hotting up. Hard on his heels another fitter came along, as his job was complete; so I asked him to fit a new graduable brake valve and a set of 'pop' safety valves on No. 7611, which was lying in the shed. This engine was a V1 2–6–2 tank which had been constructed at Doncaster in 1935 and subsequently rebuilt as a V3 in 1953. She was always based at

Parkhead to which she had come when new and thus No. 7611 was very much one of our family. We had all these fittings in our store, but there was a snag with the brake: the type on the engine was a Mark I variety whereas the set in the store was Mark II. I could assure the fitter that the piping was the same, and so he must just 'get it bunged on'. It was only ten days before that we had had the same problem, but some folk's memories are short!

It was time now to see if the board had been marked up. I noted that the 7.35 p.m. 'conditional' had been 'caped' which was a code word for put in suspension. Meantime I found out that one of our big engines, a B1, had been returned as 'not steaming'. I was well aware that the pair who had taken her out in the forenoon could contrive to loose steam standing still. Nevertheless, I sent for Jimmy and together we examined the smokebox and just about everything else. We could find nothing wrong. In these circumstances I would leave word for the night driver who would come on duty at 9.15 p.m. – that would give us a second opinion.

It was time now to have a look at the Black Five; for some reason we always called them 'hikers' in Scotland. The spring had been renewed but I could see that the clip supporting the feed pipe from the tender was too long and allowed the feed bag to rub on the brake shaft. Although the feed bag was armoured the job was just not good enough. I told Jimmy to shorten it by boring a set of new holes.

By this time almost half the shift had gone past. I collected fresh repair cards and welcomed another 'teas up' from the timekeeper, for this was a meal break. While we were in the middle of eating our 'pieces', the steam raiser looked in to say that an engine was 'showing false water'. This could be serious and ever since the deplorable accident to *Fury* there were firm instructions regarding the methods of dealing with it. Actually two types of gauge cocks were used on boilers – first Klinger cocks in which the test cocks worked in a sleeve packing which was easily renewed, and could be repaired in ten minutes. The other variety was the Dewrance cock which was packed with an asbestos compound; this could only be renewed at the works as the complete test cock had to be replaced. I went at once to the locomotive myself and found that it was a Klinger cock. There and then I made up my mind to renew the sleeve myself, which would ensure that it would be done to my satisfaction and be my responsibility.

By 7 p.m. the evening goods were being prepared for the road; up to 10 p.m. there were two main line express goods, two trains of coal empties for the Lothian area, and three 'short roads' pilots – in other words engines which ran trains from one yard to another and contrived to do a bit of shunting here and there – plus three 'conditionals'. The examiner had only discovered minor jobs requiring attention and so the men could easily keep on top of the work. The team on the washout engines were having a quiet time too.

At 9.30 p.m. a shout from the timekeeper sent me hurrying to his office; he was on the phone and scribbling on a pad: "We'll need the tool van for X2 yard – a real pitch in there – the engine is derailed with all wheels off the road – five vans are off as well, and two wagons smashed up". A quick consultation with the running foreman showed that his first set of men for the tool van engine would not be available until 10.15 p.m. Four of my lads agreed to stay on. They went up to the van to light the fire and make some tea, while we sent for the tool van attendant.

Back in the office I found my relief had arrived. "What sort of day has it been?" "Fairly quiet, it's all in the book, and by the way, the tool van's going out at 10.30 p.m. – there's a derailment up the road. Four men are staying on to help – so it's all yours, chum".

As you can see my job called for instant decision making, and there was always the come back, "The leading fitter told me to do this or that". Much of the work might seem repetitive, but it was not really so. A renewal of brake cylinder bolts, for example, was normally a simple enough task but it might set us unexpected problems. There might be no correct bolts in the store, and that is where improvisation came into the picture. This was the secret of successful work at a running shed. In the works with regular hours and a store with everything to hand, or else machines to make it, people could never appreciate the difficulties of shed fitters. Seven days a week we stayed where the action was, in spite of unsocial hours in order to keep the wheels on the railways turning. Job satisfaction came not from thanks or letters of commendation but from the fact that when our turn was over we could look at the shift sheets showing that our locomotives were 'all out on time'. There was the oft-repeated tale of the shed where the locomotives' slow starts were as common as rainy days. The story ran that one evening three engines in a row left *on time* and the whole staff were so tickled with this rare event that they ran a lap of honour right round the shed!

Many of the locomotives which I knew at Parkhead were suitable either for passenger or goods workings. It had become customary to build engines which quickly earned the title 'mixed-traffic'. Some of these classes were turned out in hundreds, one of the earliest mass-produced varieties being the former L.N.W.R. 'DX' class 0–6–0s. These could be used in all sorts of situations even where the engines were called upon to perform work which was not their usual metier.

Following upon the 1923 Grouping, the L.M.S.R. introduced several types of mixed-traffic locomotive. First of all there were the 4Fs, which were based on the former Midland Railway 0–6–0s. Over 575 of these were built between 1924 and 1941; they were to be found all over the L.M.S. system.

In 1926 a start was made in turning out 245 2–6–0 engines that from their somewhat ungainly appearance earned the nickname 'Crabs', but up in Scotland we always knew them as Moguls. They were used very extensively on passenger excursion trains, where their 5ft. 6in. driving wheels proved to be no handicap to speed.

The *pièce de résistance,* however, was the introduction in 1934 of the Stanier designed 'Class 5' 4–6–0s. These engines were being built right up to 1950. The final total for the class came to 842 locomotives and over the years they won an enviable reputation for ease of working, reliability and strength. A well known writer referrred to the Class 5s as the engines that 'won the war', scarcely mentioning all the other hard working locomotives in existence. The Class 5s certainly caught enthusiasts' imaginations and so far about a dozen of them have been preserved.

The Great Western also developed standard designs of steam engine to a degree unequalled on any other line. Their principal mixed-traffic class could be said to be the 'Hall' 4–6–0s; these could handle almost any type of work which came their way. On the L.N.E.R., however, the actual number of mixed-traffic engines did not reach large numbers, except for Thomson's B1 4–6–0s which amounted to some 400.

Readers in years to come may wonder what exactly a mixed-traffic engine did. Let me enlighten you by quoting from an actual roster for a week's working by an L.M.S. 'hiker' or Black Five. Once these engines became 'common users' they wandered all over the system; a locomotive normally based at Perth might turn up at Crewe or even farther afield.

*Monday* At 4 a.m. the engine worked a fast goods from Perth to Carlisle arriving at 11 a.m. and went to the shed for servicing. At 2.30 p.m. it piloted a passenger train from Carlisle to Crewe, arriving at 5.20 p.m.; then went off to the shed for servicing.

At 9 p.m. it took a fast goods from Crewe to Willesden, arriving at 4.40 a.m.

*Tuesday* After servicing at the shed, it set off at 7 a.m. on a slow passenger train from Euston to Birmingham; then to the shed for servicing, where it was discovered that the boiler was due for washing-out, and so the locomotive was sent 'light engine' to Crewe shed from where the information had originally come.

Wednesday The boiler wash-out took place and any repair work was done.

Thursday After the engine had been steamed, it ran to Carlisle, piloting the Mid-day Scot. After arrival there around 8 p.m., it was re-serviced and sent to Perth on a fast goods, which left Carlisle about 1.30 a.m.

Friday Arriving at Perth at 9 a.m. the engine was serviced and left on a passenger train for Inverness about 3.30 p.m. It was remanned at Aviemore. On arrival at Inverness it was retained until Saturday forenoon to work a van train to Perth.

Saturday The engine took the vans of fish and whisky freight to Perth, where it was put in the shed for the weekend to be prepared for the following week's working.

This was an accepted type of programme for a Black Five during the years of intensive 'common user' activity. Some railway enthusiasts told me about visiting Greenock shed one weekend and finding five 'hikers' there, none of which was based at Greenock; they came from such far-away places as Crewe, Llandudno, Bletchley and Liverpool.

At a depot such as Perth, whenever an engine came out of the shops and was in first-class condition, the staff would hold on to it as long as possible, utilising it in the following way. It would be allocated to two sets of men. Crew No. 1 would work an early train to Glasgow, returning with a Glasgow – Aberdeen train. After the engine was remanned at Perth by Crew No. 2, it would go on to Aberdeen, returning later that day with either a passenger or fish train, which would be taken south from Perth by another engine. The Perth engine then rested in the shed until the following day's action commenced. An average weekly mileage of between 1 500 and 2 000 miles was soon run up – enough to satisfy the statistics experts.

Sheds that could indulge in such arrangements were relatively few in number for there were depots where the daily workings were so awkward that a system of 'first in, soonest out' was followed irrespective of where the engine was likely to land.

There were regrettable features of the 'common user' period. If an engine crew arrived at say Carlisle well over their regular hours of duty they might be relieved there, handing the engine over to another team. If they then suffered the same problem at, say, Crewe, the depot there would have no compunction in reservicing the locomotive and sending it off on other wanderings in preference to one of their own engines.

During the Second World War, lodging turns were stopped and system of engine crews swopping over with other men on the road w. introduced. This led to considerable friction with the trade unions. passenger or freight train might leave Carlisle for Crewe with changeover planned to take place at Preston. An engine crew migl indulge in a bit of loafing about somewhere and knock out tl changeover point, thus compelling the Carlisle team to travel furth afield. These fellows would subsequently demand relief on the retur journey, possibly at Carnforth, and so travel home 'on the cushions', a it was termed. Enginemen had regrets about the absence of lodgin turns, as they lost mileage payments.

Shed foremen had to cope as best they could with these situations an try to keep the railway moving. The operating departments ofte seemed to think that those of us who were on the motive power sid were a gang of rascals out to make mischief for them. Shed foreme were sure to find that 'the buck was passed to them and stayed there Not only had they to know the ins and outs of all the workings, bt also the intricacies of union agreements, both national and local, whic could be the cause of staff problems.

To give an example of these agreements, enginemen had to have a 1 hours rest period between shifts. A spare set of men due out at 2 a.m could not be called at 1 a.m., although there was general agreement tha a set of men could have their shift times varied by up to four hours usually reckoned two hours either way. The 2 a.m. crew were thu barred by the 12 hour rest period from any variation in their startin time of 2 a.m. Rules of this type were seized upon by what we calle the 'mess room lawyers', who created trouble out of a foreman's hones attempts to find a solution agreeable to all. Nevertheless it was a jo with a challenge. Each turn of duty brought fresh problems rarely real ised by either railway enthusiasts or the travelling public. In these cir cumstances our mixed-traffic engines often came to our rescue.

My work sometimes required me to travel on the footplate. An en gine in steam became alive and sentient, yet few people could appreciat what working on a footplate was like. Members of the public rarely ha the opportunity to accompany enginemen with locomotives on the road. If any enthusiasts went 'footplating' they had to tolerate the pres ence of an inspector who in most instances cramped the style of th two enginemen.

If one stood at night on an overbridge to watch the line when a fas train passed below, one might glimpse the train crew at work in the cal – the fireman might be attending to the fire. Did onlookers ever won-er what it was like to shovel three or four tons of coal into the firebox during a three-hour run? All this while attempting to stand on a rocking, swaying, floor travelling at 60 to 70 miles per hour; in addition, the fireman had to keep an eye on the water and assist the driver to watch the road.

On the left hand side of the cab, the onlooker would see the driver – standing, or maybe sitting, although that might be anything but comfortable – looking ahead for his only guide – the signals glowing green when the road was clear, and red when something was wrong somewhere. At the moment the source of the trouble would be unknown to him; only the watchful men in the signalboxes would have that knowledge.

Engine driving was a matter of concentration to an extent unimagined by ordinary travellers. The signals had to be strictly observed; the driver had to have a close acquaintance with the road; the timing of the train had to be watched. The driver had to supervise the work of his mate and the performance of the engine. In many ways he could be likened to the skipper of a ship.

The good driver's senses were attuned to the rhythmic working of the engine, and he could tell almost instinctively if anything was amiss. Conversation on the footplate was minimal – due to the din from the locomotive in action as much as from the fact that the enginemen had a job to do which required concentration and effort. All this made sustained discussion on any topic practically impossible. I always knew that the thrill of fast, safe travel on the line arose from the self discipline of the engine crew. Enginemen could make driving sound easy.

Jock McLeish once recounted a story about the driver of a Crewe–Perth train who was taken ill at Perth. He had to be sent home with his fireman during the day. Jock and his mate were therefore called out to work the night train to Carlisle with an L.M.S. Pacific. At Carlisle the engine was to be remanned by a team of Crewe men. After an uneventful journey south, the Perth enginemen arrive at the Citadel station. A bright, breezy youngish man stepped on to the footplate with a "Well, driver, any problems?" Jock looked at him for a moment, and then said, "Nae problems, lad, efter you've been as lang on the job as me, you'll jist sit doon on that seat, an' open up that hanle, an' ca' awa. When you want to stop, you'll shut aff, an' apply the brake, an' you'll get to Crewe aricht. Noo, she's a' yours". So saying Jock got off with his fireman to make for home!

Every locomotive had its own character: even engines of the same class felt different to drive, and each required special attention if they were to give of their best. Some locomotives moved in a thoroughly awkward fashion. The L.N.E.R. 'Shires' had a curious gait, rather a 'leg at each corner' in action, if you ask me. The movement on the footplate was also peculiar. They swayed and undulated all over the place – so much so that enginemen coming off Shires after long hauls had a staggering gait – 'shire legs' they called it. The unpleasant movements were attributed to the coil springs. It was, therefore, a tough assignment to fire a Shire. The trick was to 'pit a ton oan her' when the train was standing in the station prior to setting out, for there was little possibility of putting coal on the fire once the engine was in motion! Churchward's County class 4–4–0s were also accused of similar behaviour, while the L.N.W.R. George V class could be really rough at times too. Former G.N.S.R. men up in Scotland's north-east loathed any ex-N.B.R. Glens which came their way. Why? These locomotives also had coil rather than leaf springs, to which the engine crews were accustomed.

Occasionally, we had visitors to our running shed. Some were friends who were knowledgeable and courteous, as well as eager to learn. They took photographs and jotted notes about our locomotives. It was only in the 1960s that the peculiar word 'gricer' first came to my attention, and I must confess that its meaning escaped me. Then an acquaintance gave me a clue: the term seemed to apply to a special variety of railway enthusiast who was festooned with cameras and tape-recording apparatus; these gricers trailed with great persistence after steam-hauled trains which were by then becoming relatively rare.

Over the years I came into contact with many other railway enthusiasts. There was a minority (a very small minority at that) who were interested in the mechanical details of motive power and rolling stock. There were those who were absorbed by railway history, and there were a large number who seemed preoccupied only with 'cops' which, being translated, means the collection of the numbers carried by engines and rolling stock. Those most concerned with number collecting were the genuine gricers.

No journey appeared too arduous or lengthy for the gricer intent upon observing steam locomotives. I recollect an afternoon when I was on duty at Parkhead when a bus load of the gricer species arrived. They tore round the premises in a little over ten minutes! One bright fellow who took time to ask how many of our engines were out working and where they might be seen, blithely informed me that they had 'done' twenty four sheds that day! I was truly amazed at the outpouring of energy on such an exercise.

At a time when steam haulage was becoming infrequent, I remember travelling from Leeds to Glasgow over one of the scenic lines in the

North of England, the Settle to Carlisle route. I was puzzled by the large gatherings of people with their cars and cycles by the lineside at Aisgill and other places until an attendant told me that the crowds were waiting for a steam excursion to pass! Points such as Scout Green, the small signalbox on Shap, were also thronged by enthusiasts who turned up at weekends in their hundreds to catch sight of any steam hauled trains. Far from diminishing, these activities have been increasing, with steam specials now being a feature of British Rail excursions as well as there being regular services on numerous preserved lines. As main line traction becomes increasingly stereotyped so will railway enthusiasts seek variety, colour and excitement wherever steam engines run.

The preserved engines are magnificently kept; they perform like sewing machines, and have attention lavished upon them. Once having turned out two engines for an enthusiasts' excursion – and I must say I thought the locomotives looked quite impressive – doubts were forcibly expressed about my parentage as well as that of the engines. Apparently their appearance left something to be desired. Well, one cannot win all the time.

# CHAPTER TEN

## *Envoi*

RAILWAY ENTHUSIASTS HAVE sometimes asked me this question, "What was your most memorable journey?" That is an easy one to answer, as the following account of an extraordinary journey will show. Although high speeds were common on the Strathmore route, I once experienced exceptionally slow progress over it. This was the result of the national railway strike, which began on Friday 26th September 1919. As the afternoon wore on both sides were still holding out and no settlement was reached. The Strike was on!

I had been told to go north to Aberdeen in connection with my work on the Caley. Although I could have travelled by day, it seemed to me that a journey around midnight when the strike was timed to commence might be more eventful. I must admit that the thought of a stranding somewhere along the line never entered my youthful head. I chose to travel by the 10 p.m. from Buchanan Street station, Glasgow, which was due into Perth by 12 p.m.

On my arrival at Buchanan Street, a large notice board proclaimed 'Passengers for North of Perth may be unable to complete their journey'. An inspector was interviewing such passengers; as a result some turned away while others chose to travel.

When I made my way to the front of the train, I found that McIntosh

4-4-0 No. 119 of Perth shed was waiting in charge of old friends of mine, driver George Smith and fireman Willie Chapman. They hailed me with a mock air of disapproval, but when I asked the driver if he thought we would get to Perth, he replied, 'Och aye, we'll get hame aricht!' This gave me fresh optimism.

Promptly at 10 p.m. came a loud hoot on the whistle and No. 119 set off with only about 50 passengers on the train. At Larbert we were joined by a party of anglers, going to Perthshire for a weekend's fishing. They had clearly been celebrating and were in uproarious mood. A melodeon was produced and an extensive repertoire of Scottish airs and songs kept us entertained. At Stirling, some passengers alighted and the two coaches for Oban were detached before the train left again.

Our arrival at Gleneagles was scheduled for 11.45 p.m. or so, but from then on progress would very much depend on what took place in the signalboxes. The unions had told their signalmen members to switch out at midnight and set all signals at danger. There was a real possibility of being held up on the main line if this action was taken. We duly stopped at Gleneagles and stood for some time, which allowed me to go out to speak to Driver Smith – he was still quite convinced that we would reach Perth. He had heard that an inspector was in charge at Hilton Junction box outside Perth, and that the station masters were having to man any other boxes that were required.

After a longish wait we left again, this time at a very modest pace, and while we were going through Dunning I was amused to see Willie Chapman cleaning out the fire and dumping it on the lineside.

Soon the train was passing Hilton Junction; once through Moncrieff tunnel, a slow run past the engine sheds brought our train into the down main line platform, where No. 119 was promptly uncoupled. The engine pulled into an adjoining loop where the fireman filled the boiler and Driver Smith took off the regulator handle, locked it in the tool box and gave the key to an inspector.

Meanwhile an Aberdeen engine which was lying ahead of our train backed up and coupled on. This was another McIntosh 4-4-0, No. 44, with driver Alan Middleton and fireman Charlie Tough from Ferryhill. This crew had brought the 7.30 p.m. sleeper from Aberdeen to Perth, and were due to return with the 12.50 a.m. Perth to Aberdeen – this train combined the 10 p.m. from Glasgow, and the Aberdeen portion of the 8.34 p.m. from Carlisle (which had started out as the 2 p.m. from Euston, no less).

Perth station was surprisingly busy: passengers for the south were milling about, while the fishermen were engaged in yet another impromptu concert in the waiting room. Apart from our Caley engine No. 44, the only other locomotive in steam was a Highland 4-4-0T; the fireman and the driver were having an argument about drawing the fire. Eventually matters were settled when an inspector took it off to the Highland shed.

As it was after midnight, the signalboxes were now manned by those staff members qualified to work them. About 1.15 a.m. a shout came from the Centre box, "The Corridor's coming. We'll shove him in the up main", and into the station came No. 896, a Carlisle engine, driven by J. Lawson of Kingmoor shed.

Meanwhile, on No. 44, Alan Middleton and his mate were discussing their own situation. If they were to use the engine to get home then they might as well take the train with the passengers; if they did not take the train, they might as well leave and let the union find some way of getting them home. Shortly, Driver Middleton, some railway officials and union representatives left for an office to discuss what should be done. I tagged on behind, and found that my presence was unnoticed by the 'big shots'. The group was soon phoning Glasgow for advice, although it occurred to me that there would be enough problems in that area without any others coming from Perth that night!

After an interval, I strolled back to No. 44, where Charlie Tough was entertaining about six children on the footplate. They were sitting on a plank drinking tea, which he had somehow procured for them. What an adventure this was for these youngsters!

It was now about 3 a.m. Charlie Tough had uncoupled the Inverness portion of the train, but kept the three Aberdeen coaches attached to his engine. He had put on the steam heating and the majority of the passengers for Aberdeen were trying to catch some sleep. The anglers were still entertaining those who were about, but as time went on they too became tired and Perth station grew quiet. I went back to see how Alan Middleton was fairing: but there was still no decision – Glasgow would not give any lead. Officials had to be certain that the line was open to Aberdeen and, in any case, the running of the train might mean trouble with the men on strike – this latter possibility weighed heavily with staff. Driver Middleton thought, however, that he would have few problems.

As I was cold I went back to No. 44; the fireman had put the youngsters into the train, and while I gave him the latest news, I got into a corner of the cab where it was warm. Then Charlie said to me, "You look after her for a while – I'm going to stretch my legs". He went off the footplate and I dozed in my corner; after a snooze I looked at my watch – it was 4.30 a.m. I put on the injector and shovelled some coal nto the firebox. Just as I finished, Charlie came back. "We're off at 6 .m. – only the passengers from Glasgow and Carlisle are going north n the train; we don't exceed 25 miles an hour and we lift no-one".

When Alan Middleton arrived, his only comment was "We'll get here sometime", and the enginemen set about their tasks. At 6.03 a.m. he resonant hoot from the whistle was heard again; and slowly the rain pulled out, only to stop at Balhousie box. The chap in the box nerely informed the crew that their first manned point was Stanley unction box, and we restarted. It was a lovely fresh morning; people y the lineside stared at the train in case, as someone said, it was a long ime before they saw its like again!

At Stanley, a Highland goods for Perth hauled by a Jones 4–6–0 was t a standstill, while the crew amused themselves by playing quoits with some iron rings. After the man in the box had a chat with our lriver we went on to Coupar Angus, stopping at Ardler and Alyth on he way. At Coupar some of the staff on strike were gathered at the ence near the South box watching the stationmaster operate it, before roceeding to the North cabin. Some good-natured chaffing took place etween them and the engine crew. The stationmaster was given an ronic cheer as he left the box, and a reminder that by virtue of his resent duties it was his turn to clean the signalbox windows!

We started off again making for Forfar, where a solitary 0–4–4 tank tood in a siding at Forfar South – fire out, regulator handle off, and ocked up. We coasted slowly into the station, drawing up at the water olumn. While Charlie saw to the filling of the tank, and shovelled lown coal, Driver Middleton and some of the passengers went off to a nearby baker's shop to buy some food. It was about 10.30 a.m. and ong past time for breakfast; the stationmaster's wife brought milk for he children. Her husband had to spend some time with our driver and he local strikers who were in an argumentative mood. They were quite bjectionable to our train crew, but tempers mercifully cooled and a ailwayman fetched a large jug of tea for the enginemen and guard.

About 11 a.m. we left for Dubton Junction, where we found a Glas-zow-bound goods train standing in the up loop. The enginemen had ut the fire out and were sitting forlornly in the station. After some rgument the local stationmaster reluctantly agreed to their travelling ack to Aberdeen with us, although strict orders had been given that no assengers were to be taken on board.

Kinnaber box was occupied by an inspector who waved us through, nd from then on we stopped at every station. At Laurencekirk I was mused to see a southbound North British goods lying in a loop, its rew sound asleep on the embankment! About 1 p.m. we overtook a

Caley goods engine going north light. Its crew had apparently reached Bridge of Dun just after midnight and, after waiting there until 9 a.m or so, they were told to take their engine back to Aberdeen.

From Stonehaven we jogged along the coast until the granite spires o Aberdeen came into view, glittering in the brilliant light. Past Craig inches and over the river, where the driver gave a peculiar 'three hoot' whistle (which I later learned was his signal to his family at home), and we rolled into No. 6 platform at exactly 2.20 p.m. – over 16 hours from the commencement of the journey!

I went up to No. 44 just as my footplate friends were leaving her; an inspector told them, "Awa' hame noo lads – ye've done well". They certainly had – it was now 2.30 p.m. and they had booked on at 6.15 p.m. the previous evening! Outside the locked gates of the station a sizeable crowd had gathered – strikers, police, pickets, and the usual groups of what are today called 'rubber-necks'.

As the two enginemen with the guard, plus the handful of passenger. left the station a great cheer went up from the people outside. Alan Middleton looked puzzled; he probably felt *we* ought to be cheering since we had reached home at last. At the gate the passengers thanked our engine crew, and this greatly embarrassed them. A stout matron insisted on kissing them both, which brought forth the comment from Charlie, "Heaven help us if the wife hears aboot this!"

As I made my way out my mind went back to that day in 1895 when John Souter and his engine No. 17 made the famous dash from Perth to Aberdeen in the Railway Races. He set up a record that has never been equalled, but Alan Middleton set up another sort of record for the same stretch of track – over 8 hours for 90 miles, and likewise while pulling a tiny train!

Everyone I suppose has a favourite locomotive; but there was one locomotive in Scotland that was a legend. It was the mighty *Cardean* – the phrase is not of my selection – it was first written by enthusiastic journalists in 1906, the year in which No. 903 came from St. Rollox works. Mighty the locomotive was, for it was the biggest on any Scottish railway at that time. I have a special affection for the engine, as it was the first on which I was set to work.

To those to whom *Cardean* is but a name, it is almost impossible to imagine the aura about it, or the interest people took in this giant among locomotives. The name was that of the Perthshire estate of the Caley's vice chairman. The large chime whistle, which may have been a ship's siren, was brought from America. No. 903's principal employment was to haul the Caley prestige trains – the 2 p.m. 'Up Corridor' for London as far as Carlisle, returning with the 'Down Corridor' from that city in the evening. Of course, the Caley was a publicity-conscious line – tin plate models of the engine were on sale at the booking offices at 2/6d! Press photographs taken at the time of the inaugural runs show the 2 p.m. leaving Glasgow Central with opposite platform thick with people simply there to watch the spectacle!

At the commencement, the engine crew were driver James Currie and fireman James Watson of Glasgow; week after week these men were on this top working. James Currie was on the footplate when *Cardean* met with a broken driving axle near Crawford Station. The cause was metal fatigue. He went on to become a locomotive inspector; his replacement was named Gibson, a rather flamboyant character who was only too willing to assist with publicity for the engine and its train.

The stories that grew up about No. 903 were legion; while some were certainly correct, many were just fables! For example, men spoke of the lurch which the engine always gave when it went past the scene of the Crawford failure. Nearer the truth was the story of the little farmhouse by the line, where every evening the farmer and his wife came out to wave to the enginemen. In winter they shone a storm lantern – both salutes receiving an anwer – a blast on the powerful whistle!

Kipling once wrote that 'romance brought up the 5.15', but there was certainly romance in the hauling of the 8.13 from Carlisle north. For years Carlisle station was the evening setting for scenes similar to those in Glasgow Central at lunch time. Let us go back to those years. About 7.15 p.m., the 2 p.m. from Euston pulls into the down main line platform. Very often it has taken two London & North Western engines to bring it up Shap. These are quickly uncoupled from the train, and run onto the adjoining line. In the twilight, a huge blue tender can be seen coasting in to couple on to the stationary coaches. With a slight bump, the Caley engine arrives on top of the train. The fireman clambers gingerly below the buffers to couple the engine to the coaches, every movement being watched by the throng of onlookers.

Meanwhile one of the train guards comes up to speak to the driver, giving him the weight of the train, plus the usual 'chaff' that always takes place. Once the driver has tested the brakes, checking over the gauges, he gives a sign to his fireman who then climbs on to the tender to await the flash of a white light from the guard. The fireman waves a flare lamp in reply to signify that the brakes are working. All is quiet now, save for the hissing of the impatient engine and the slow panting of the Westinghouse pump. Then there is a flurry of activity: a faint crashing noise comes from up front – it is the arm of the advance starting signal changing from red to green. Now everyone waits for the right away from the guard. The fireman comes on to the platform; he is watching the rear of the train. Shortly a whistle shrills; then a green light flashes from the tail of the train. The fireman shouts "Right-o, mate!", then with a resonant blast on its siren, *Cardean* moves majestically north. The station clock points to 8.13 p.m. – on time again. To the spectators on the platform the excitement is over for another night. Some enthusiasts came almost every evening to see the famous engine set out for Glasgow.

Although the 'Corridors' were prestige trains, their timings were scarcely spectacular. Over the years little acceleration in the workings took place. In 1908 the train left Glasgow Central at 2 p.m. travelling non-stop to Carlisle, arriving at 4.15 p.m. In the evening it left Carlisle at 8.13 p.m. running non-stop to Beattock where there was a halt for a banker at 8.57 p.m., the train passing the summit at 9.18 p.m. After a pause at Strawfrank Junction to put off the coaches for Edinburgh, it came into Glasgow Central at 10.20 p.m. So the gentlemen's agreement about the 8½ hour journey from the capital was almost kept!

The timings were much the same as those in force in 1900, although by 1908 the coaches were the heavy 65′ West Coast Joint Stock. The composition of the train was as follows:—

Brake Third, Restaurant Car, Composite, Brake Third; Brake Third plus Composite for Liverpool, Restaurant Car (taken off at Preston); Composite with Brake Third for Manchester. The 'Up Corridor' was thus nine coaches long, but the 'Down' was only seven in length.

When one recalls *Cardean's* great achievements on the L.N.W.R. route in June/July 1909, it is surprising that the timing of the trains was not re-thought, especially after the engine was given a superheater in 1911. This brought about a transformation in its performance. It is a pity that there was no repetition of the tests on the L.N.W.R. Timings apart, the engine was the best-known on any Scottish line – people who knew no other locomotive became quite emotional at the mention of the name.

I like in fancy to stand somewhere on those bare moors near Beattock Summit about 9.30 p.m. of a summer's evening. Through the soft air one may hear in the gentle 'sough' the full throat of a chime whistle far away. In the eyes of memory, I can see again a great blue engine hurtling north with its string of palatial white-and-lake coaches. Re-echoing from the heather hills comes the clicking of wheels over rail joints. 'True to time, true to time, true to time', they say. Yes, the Corridor is coming north on time. . . .